STAR AND PLANET SPOTTING

Star and Planet Spotting

A Field Guide to the Night Sky

Peter Lancaster Brown

BLANDFORD PRESS

Poole   Dorset

First published in the U.K. 1974
by Blandford Press, Link House, West Street,
Poole, Dorset BH15 1LL

Copyright © 1974 Blandford Books Ltd

Reprinted 1981

ISBN 0 7137 0655 4

To *all stargazers—young and old*

Printed in the U.S.A.

Contents

Ursa Major, the key to northern constellations.

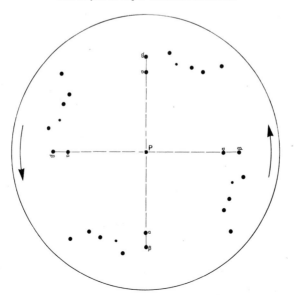

Acknowledgements

The author and publisher gratefully acknowledge the following sources for photographs and colour illustrations.

Mt Wilson and Palomar Observatories, Plates 3, 4, 5, 6, 7, 8, 11; Figs. 6, 7, 8, 39, 45, 48, 52, p. 8. United States Naval Observatory, Plates 2, 9, 10, 12. Australian News and Information Bureau, Fig. 47. Royal Astronomical Society, Figs. 49, 51. Tokyo Observatory, Fig. 50. American Meteorite Laboratory, Fig. 53. John Wood, Plate 13.

The author wishes to thank the staff of Blandford Press for their continued enthusiasm and helpfulness in all matters and his wife, Johanne, for her usual generous and unflagging assistance.

Preface

THE study of antiquity has shown that astronomy has a special place in the history of human culture, and that stars and sky-lore were certainly the most influential factors of early science.

Again, in contemporary times, astronomy has become one of the most dominant sciences affecting human thinking; the launching of artificial satellites and space probes despatched to the Moon and planets have brought the man in the street, via the popular press and television, face to face with the very frontiers of knowledge. Perhaps for the first time many ordinary citizens have wandered outdoors to see a satellite or spent rocket traversing the heavens and then speculated about the names of some of the brighter background stars and planets and the reason why the ancient astronomers formed romantic legends and myths about them. The English writer Carlyle wistfully echoed many a person's frustrations when he wrote: 'Why did not somebody teach me the constellations and make me at home in the starry heavens?'

Long before the invention of clocks and watches, the ancient races used the stars as timekeepers. In a play by Euripides a character asks: 'What is the star now passing?' To which came the reply: 'The Pleiades show themselves in the east, the Eagle (Aquila) soars in the Summit of the heavens.'

Nowadays, although most people have no need of star knowledge for daily living, many, nevertheless, still succumb to the fascination and beauty of the night sky. As a hobby, even simple star and planet spotting provides a never-ending source of interest and satisfaction.

A working familiarity with the brighter stars and planets is not difficult to acquire. A few evenings outdoors, in conjunction with a study of the star maps and charts, will soon whet the appetite to borrow or buy a pair of binoculars to view the myriad celestial objects just at the limit or beyond the limit of naked-eye visibility.

Astronomy as a universal science appeals to people in different ways. It can be a practical study conducted outdoors where the stars, planets and other celestial objects can be viewed and studied in their natural setting. But for those with little or no inclination or opportunity for outdoor observation it can also be a stimulating pastime studied secondhand—much like the armchair traveller enjoys browsing through maps and narratives about exploration and travel. This book is written for both these audiences.

PETER LANCASTER BROWN

The Night Sky

THE first watchers of the sky imagined the celestial sphere as a roof or vault on which the heavenly bodies were studded and represented as lying together side by side on its inner surface. Even Omar Khayyam (1017–1123), the astronomer-poet of Persia, wrote: 'that inverted bowl we call the sky'. Today, although our ideas about the Universe are very different, it is still convenient for star and planet spotting purposes to treat the heavens as a large, inverted, star-studded hemispherical bowl.

The grouped star patterns, or constellations, are as old as, if not older than, the first civilizations, and no one is sure who first formed them. We do know, however, that many of the constellation patterns we recognize today were in use in Babylonia over 4,000 years ago, and these in turn had been borrowed from the much earlier Sumerian culture.

The first full description of the constellations is recorded in the *Phenomena*, a poem written by Aratus of Soli about 280 B.C. But Aratus was a poet, not an astronomer, and his work is simply a versification of an astronomical work by Eudoxus dated 370 B.C., unfortunately now lost. Aratus provides us with an account of the forty-eight constellations recognized by the Greeks. Whenever mention is made of 'the ancient forty-eight constellations', this refers to the ones cited by Aratus.

Later cultures and civilizations, which borrowed the forty-eight constellations from their Middle Eastern source, adopted and modified them according to their own imaginations. Whereas the Greeks in their groups alluded mostly to animal figures such as Aries, the Ram; Taurus, the Bull; Gemini, the Twins (or goats, which give birth to twins), some eastern races introduced earrings, razors, pieces of coral, plus other more whimsical and mundane objects.

Elsewhere in the world other civilizations invented their own constellations. The Chinese in particular formed many star asterisms, and these often perpetuated the titles of their bureaucratic civil servants. In pre-Columbian America, the Maya, Aztecs, Incas, and their associated cultures made considerable use of the stars. Pre-Columbian astronomy was very advanced, but unfortunately little is known about it owing to the wholesale destruction of nearly all original source material by the Conquistadors. Much of our present astronomical knowledge about these advanced civilizations is based on a handful of codices and monuments, which escaped destruction by the Spaniards.

But it was not only the 'civilized' societies which formed constellations and invented romantic mythological stories about the stars and planets. Primitive races as far afield as the Eskimoes of the Greenland Ice Cap and the Aborigines of Australia have studied the heavens since earliest times, and much of their nature philosophy and religion is based on stories woven round celestial bodies.

Modern man's Paleolithic ancestors probably had an excellent working knowledge of the movements of the Sun, Moon, stars, and planets—certainly more than our immediate Victorian and Edwardian forebears realized when they used terms like 'Barbarians' and 'Savages' to describe these ancient races. Although in early times written languages were not yet invented, some ancient artefacts show quite unambiguously that numeration and notation systems were in wide usage. In this way Paleolithic man kept tally of the Moon's phases and the rising and setting of prominent stars to foretell the coming and the passage of the seasons.

In north-west Europe in Megalithic times, about 4,000 years ago, huge stone circles were constructed—such as Avebury and Stonehenge in Britain—which we now realize had profound astronomical significance. By using standing stones as markers, these ancient men were able to predict the rising and setting of stars and the movements of the Sun and Moon with astonishing accuracy. It was in this way that the calendar of the early Neolithic farmers was regulated.

Thus, as we can see, star and planet spotting is no new occupation, for it represented the first 'intellectual' activity of mankind on our planet. We can read in the ancient Egyptian and Babylonian texts that the sky revealed itself as an awesome presence—suggestive of an omniscient power so great that it commanded allegiance simply by its appearance. To the Egyptians the star-studded night sky created a kind of 'welling up' of man's soul and made him realize his own insignificance in the scheme of nature. Today, in spite of man's almost total preoccupation with pursuing a materialistic life, he is still very receptive to this omniscient mood when he views 'the bowl of the night' outdoors.

In the early civilizations, astronomy and astrology were bound together as related sciences. Early astrology was considered quite respectable, especially that part of it which was concerned with periodic celestial events and the vagaries and changes of the weather. Indeed one can say that early astrology in many respects laid the foundation of the modern science of meteorology, which is still very far from being a truly 'exact' science.

It was only when astrology was applied indiscriminately to the direct affairs of men and women that its decadence began. Yet right up to the time of the seventeenth century, astrology was often more highly regarded than astronomy.

History relates that the great Kepler—who made the fundamental discovery that the planets revolved in elliptical orbits—worked for the latter in pursuit of truth but earned his daily bread by the former, and he even chose his second wife by casting horoscopes!

Although the stars and constellations are recorded on several early globes and planispheres, the first truly scientific star atlas which resembles those of the present day was the *Uranometria* of Dr Johann Bayer which he published in 1603. Bayer was the first man to adopt the present-day system of using letters of the Greek alphabet to denote the brighter stars in each constellation. Prior to this, stars were related to the constellation by some vague literal reference such as 'in the upper head Castor Apollo'. In Bayer's nomenclature this star simply became α Geminorum.★

Before Bayer made his reforms, the fainter stars were difficult to identify precisely; for example, a 5th-magnitude star taken from the same constellation of Gemini might be identified as 'in the left hand of the former twin'. It can be imagined how necessary it was for the star spotter to know his classical figures extremely well and also to be sure he was using the correct version (among several) of the imaginary classical figures in the sky. Nowadays, under Bayer's system, this star is known as θ Geminorum (or θ Gem). (*See* also Star Nomenclature, p. 20.)

Another of Bayer's reforms was to introduce the method of depicting stars on charts and globes which represented the *inside* of the celestial sphere; before this they were represented from the point of view of an observer looking inwards towards the Earth from outside the surface of the celestial sphere. The earlier method was extremely confusing, because the stars and constellation figures are reversed from what one actually sees in the sky from the surface of the Earth.

Bayer has been criticized by later astronomers for his lack of care in affixing Greek letters in strict order of brightness (magnitude). Quite often a star with the Alpha (α) designation is fainter than the Beta (β) star. Astronomers since have argued that perhaps some of the reversals in brightness are real ones, but the German astronomer Argelander, who studied the problem, concluded that Bayer was influenced in his choice by placing the Greek letters by the form and direction of the constellation. However, this still does not explain away all the anomalies.

★ Note that the Latin genitive is used when referring to a star. Thus the star Alpha (α) in the constellation Gemini becomes α Geminorum (or simply α Gem in the widely used abbreviated system).

Fig. 1   The planisphere of Philippe de la Hire of the Paris Observatory, dated 1702.

Bayer's *Uranometria* depicts sixty constellations which is an addition of twelve on the old Greek ones. Bayer had obtained his southern constellations from contemporary Dutch navigators such as Petrus Theodori (Pieter Dirckszoon Keyser) and several others. Bayer wreathes some of his stars in the traditional Greek mythological figures, but others are in contemporary late sixteenth century dress. This practice had many precedents; an Anglo-Saxon manuscript has Aratus's Perseus attired as a Saxon noble. Fig. 1 is typical of the kind of star maps which were common up to the middle of the nineteenth century. This planisphere dated 1702 uses Bayer's reforms by showing the constellation figures as seen from the surface of the Earth. However, Backer's Zodiac (Plate 1) dated 1690 still shows the figures reversed. Both these star maps are typical of the beautiful hand-coloured celestial maps of the period.

After Bayer followed many celestial map makers, some with rather radical ideas. Julius Schiller published a revision of Bayer's maps in 1627 when, instead of the latter's traditional mythological figures, he enshrined among the stars numerous Christian saints and biblical figures to replace the heathen ones. In modern times the English humourist-writer A. P. Herbert published a book entitled *A Better Sky* showing all the stars named after contemporary politicians. Needless to say, it caused considerable amusement, but fortunately that was all and was soon forgotten, as was the earlier idea when the University of Leipsic in 1807 wished to establish a lasting monument in honour of Napoleon and named the three belt stars of Orion 'the Stars of Napoleon'. Incensed Englishmen, on hearing the news, decided on the alternative title of 'the Stars of Nelson'. Neither name appears on modern star maps, which is perhaps just as well.

The Nature of Stars

OWING to the great distances of even the nearest stars,★ we are not able to observe them as resolvable discs as we do with most of the planets. No matter how large our telescope is, or how great the magnification applied, the stars remain twinkling point-blobs of light. However, by using various methods and instruments we can glean a great deal of information about their physical make-up.

Among the total population of stars in our own galaxy (the Milky Way), plus the uncountable others in the rest of the Universe, are represented a great variety of stellar objects varying in size and temperature. Some are massive bodies, or giant stars, with diameters exceeding 300 times that of our Sun (dia 1,392,000 km); others are dwarfs no larger than some of the planets in our solar system and shining so feebly that even those nearest the Sun are very faint bodies.

Although stars as a class of celestial bodies are extremely diverse, they can be classified by their various properties into types. These include White and Red Dwarfs, Subgiants, Giants and Supergiants and 'average' Main Sequence stars like our own Sun. One of the principal means of classifying stars relates to their colour, or temperature; this takes into account, along with other factors, how the star is burning up its stock of nuclear fuel and where it lies in its evolutionary path—since, like all other bodies, stars are born, evolve through various stages, and then disintegrate and die.

The hottest stars are greenish-white with surface temperatures over 40,000°C; these are followed in descending order of temperature by stars which are blue-white, white, yellowish-white, yellow (like the Sun at 6,000°C), yellow-orange, orange-red and the coolest of *visible* stars, deep red. But in addition there are even cooler stars which shine only in infrared light; these are a class of very cool Red Giants not visible in ordinary wavelengths. X-ray stars are even more bizarre objects, and likely there are other varieties of 'star' undetected by present-day instruments.

Double (and Binary) Stars

Among the vast population of stars, many which appear single to the naked

★ The nearest star, Proxima Centauri, is 4·2 light-years distant or 4·2 × 9,500,000,000,000 km (4·2 × 6,000,000,000,000 miles).

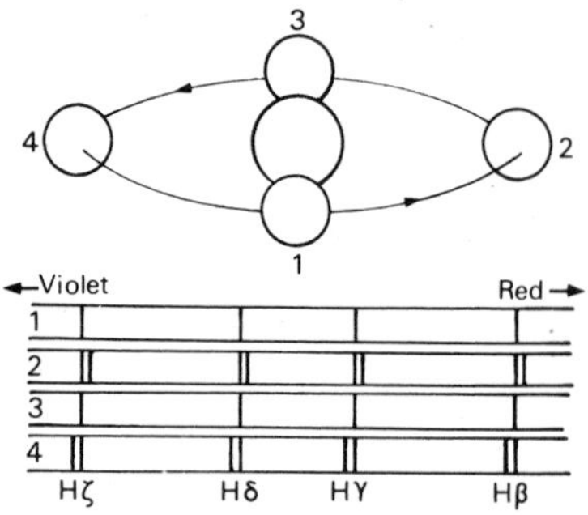

Fig. 2 *Spectroscopic binary stars can only be distinguished when examined through a spectroscope. Because of orbital motion the spectral (Fraunhofer) lines are duplicated when one star is receding from or approaching the observer and are shifted towards the red or violet ends respectively.*

eye or with low powered instruments appear double or multiple objects when examined with telescopes of moderate or high powers.

There are two kinds of double stars; true pairs called *binary stars* which have a physical connection and revolve together in orbit round a common centre of gravity; and *optical pairs* which appear double simply because two stars, by chance, lie in the observer's line of sight. Chance optical pairs may in fact be stars separated by a distance of several hundred light-years.

Among the binary pairs there are many systems where the stars are so close that through visual or photographic telescopes they cannot be separated and appear as a single star image. These stars are called *spectroscopic binaries*, because they can only be detected with an instrument called a spectroscope which splits light into its component colours and reveals as dark or bright lines the various elements contained within the light source. When we view a binary pair in the spectroscope, the chemical elements show as duplicate lines thus revealing the presence of two objects (sometimes more). By analysing the various characteristics of these telltale lines, a great deal can be deduced about each component star of such a system, and even their orbits may be calculated with a remarkable precision (*see* Fig. 2).

Variable Stars

There are many stars which do not remain at constant brightness, and their magnitudes fluctuate over a period of time—either irregularly or in precise rhythmic cycles. These cycles may be completed in a few hours, or they may take several hundred days—sometimes even longer.

Variable stars can be classified into five main divisions. These divisions exclude stars known as *secular variables* which are stars that during the course of several centuries have faded or increased in brightness in comparison with their estimated brightness recorded by earlier astronomers.

Long-Period Variables (abbreviated to LPV) are typical 'cool', orange-red or red giants. An example of this class of variable is Mira (o Cet), which at maximum brightness is visible to the naked eye (*see* p. 88). The period of the LPVs ranges between 70 and 700 days, but averages about 275 days. The regular changes in brightness are thought to occur owing to rhythmic pulsations taking place in the outer atmospheric layers of these stars.

Irregular Variables are stars often associated with nebulous material. Six groups are recognized, including red-tinted stars like 'the Garnet Star' (μ Cep) which shows minor irregular fluctuations. Another group are RV Tauri stars that resemble the eclipsing β Lyra-type variables (*see* below), but, in constrast to these latter stars, they are irregular in period.

Cepheid Variables occur in two varieties. The variations in brightness are due to short-period pulsations in the body of the star. Cepheid variables can be utilized as useful distance-measuring tools (*see* Glossary).

Eclipsing Variables are stars whose brightness variations are caused by a companion star (or stars) revolving in orbit and periodically eclipsing (or cutting off) the light of the primary star. There are two subgroups: *Algol-type stars* are so named after the prototype star Algol (β Per), 'the Demon Star' of the Arabs (*see* p. 81). The variations in brightness are characterized by well-marked minima followed by a small secondary one. β *Lyrae-type stars* are so named after the prototype star β Lyrae. These stars are ellipsoidal in shape owing to mutual gravitational interaction taking place between them. Light variations are characterized by two equal maxima with a small minimum followed by a large minimum.

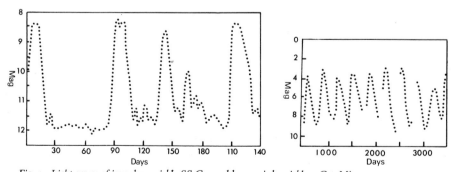

Fig. 3   Light curves of irregular variable SS Cyg and long period variable o Cet, Mira.

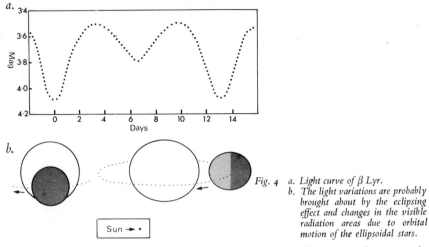

Fig. 4 *a. Light curve of β Lyr.*
b. The light variations are probably brought about by the eclipsing effect and changes in the visible radiation areas due to orbital motion of the ellipsoidal stars.

Novae (Temporary or Exploding Stars)—also sometimes known as 'new stars'. These generally represent stars which have previously been very faint objects which suddenly after a cataclysmic internal explosive event rise several magnitudes (often over 20) and become extremely brilliant objects. A rare subclass is the *supernova* which is even more brilliant but much rarer in our own galaxy. One of the most brilliant was observed by Tycho Brahe in 1572, in the constellation of Cassiopeia (*see* p. 76). Another example occurred in 1054, in Taurus, which later became the Crab Nebula, and where in recent times a visible pulsar (*see* Glossary) was detected.

A number of variable stars can be studied using the naked eye or binoculars, and some of the most interesting ones are included in the lists of deep-sky objects in each constellation (*see* pp. 74–116). A list of naked-eye variables can be found in Appendix 2 (*see* also section: Observing Variable Stars, p. 37).

Throughout the world several amateur astronomical societies and groups specialize in observing variable stars, and their members make a valuable contribution to our knowledge of these rather remarkable bodies.

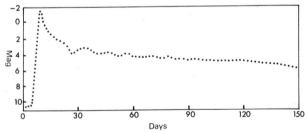

Fig. 5 Light curve of a typical nova or exploding star (Nova Aql 1918).

Fig. 6   The Horse Head nebula. The effect is caused by vast obscuring clouds of interstellar matter.

The Milky Way (The Galaxy)

All the stars we see in the night sky belong to a great single system of stars forming the local galaxy of which our own Sun is a typical, rather average, member.

When the sky is observed on a clear, moonless night—away from the city and bright street lights—a faint band of milky light appears to be concentrated in a path extending across certain constellations (*see* star maps pp. 41–45). This is what the ancient astronomers called the Milky Way about which Aratus, in his classic poem *Phenomena*, wrote: 'that shining wheel, men call it milk'. In Greek *gala* means milk, hence *Galaxy*.

The majority of the stars forming the Milky Way are located within a horizontal plane, but most of them are so distant that we cannot see them as individual points of light with the naked eye; the milky appearance is due to the effect of myriads of faint stars merged together to form a nebulous band. If it were viewed from outside in space, it would probably appear very much as the faint spiral galaxy M 31 in Andromeda (Pl. 8).

Globular Clusters are members of our galaxy and consist of aggregations of some hundreds of thousands of stars concentrated towards the centre so that their separate images appear to be fused together to suggest a continuous patch of light. Globular clusters are situated at great distances from the Sun, and the nearest is at least 20,000 light-years away. Some are well within range of binocular observations. In the northern hemisphere M 13 in Hercules

Fig. 7   The Veil Nebula, created by a supernova explosion some 50,000 years ago.

is among the best known deep-sky objects (*see* p. 79 and Pl. 2); in the southern hemisphere ω Centauri is an even brighter cluster (*see* pp. 8 and 88).

Open or Galactic Star Clusters, in contrast to globular clusters, are open, loose aggregations of stars with little or no concentration towards the centre. Generally they consist of only a few hundred stars, or less, which are arranged quite haphazardly. One of the best known and brightest is the Pleiades Cluster, or the Seven Sisters, in which at least six members are plainly visible to the naked eye, and many more in binoculars (*see* p. 103 and Pl. 6).

Galactic Nebulae are diffuse, cloud-like wisps of luminous gas, often irregular and structureless and almost entirely limited to the region of the plane of the Milky Way. Some have highly individual forms which give rise to descriptive names such as: the Horse's Head Nebula (Fig. 6); the Veil Nebula (Fig. 7); the North America Nebula (Fig. 38); and the Trifid Nebula (Pl. 4). The Orion Nebula (or the Great Nebula in Orion, M 42) is just visible to the naked eye near the star θ Orionis in 'the Sword Belt of Orion' (*see* p. 97 and Pl. 7).

Dark, Diffuse Nebulae are, as the name suggests, nebulae which are dark and not illuminated by embedded or near-by stars. As a consequence they appear as 'holes' or dark streaks—sometimes known as coal sacks—running through the star field of the Milky Way (Fig. 48).

Planetary Nebulae are so called owing to their superficial likeness to planetary discs when viewed through a telescope. Most of the examples known are quite small, and they appear as nebulous stars in small instruments. One of the most famous, the Ring Nebula in Lyra, can be seen with small telescopes and has the appearance of a delicate smoke ring (Fig. 39). Planetary nebulae are created by the explosion of a star; the famous Crab Nebula (M 1) was caused by a star which exploded in the year 1054 (Pl. 3 and p. 103).

Galaxies (Extragalactic Nebulae)

Galaxies, or extragalactic nebulae, are vast independent systems of stars situated far beyond our own Milky Way. These island universes are seen to exist in numbers uncountable and extend to the full distance and beyond the limit of detection by present-day instruments. Even the nearest of the large spirals, M 31 in Andromeda, lies at the colossal distance of 2,200,500 light-years. This object is visible to the naked eye as a small hazy cloud shining at magnitude 4, not far from the Square of Pegasus (*see* p. 97).

Galaxies appear not to be distributed over the sky in equal numbers. This is because dust in the plane of the Milky Way obscures those lying in this direction, but photographic surveys also show that galaxies appear to cluster into groups. One such group is in the constellation of Virgo, and another is in Corona Borealis (Fig. 8).

Among 'local' galaxies are the irregular-shaped Greater and Lesser Magellanic Clouds which are only visible in the southern hemisphere. These clouds are named after Magellan, the circumnavigator, who was among the first to describe them. The larger cloud has a diameter of 25,000 light-years, and the smaller one 10,000 light-years; both lie approximately 150,000 light-years distant from the Earth.

When we view spiral galaxies, we see them at different angles. Some are seen to be almost edge on, such as the Andromeda Nebula M 31 (Pl. 3).

Fig. 8   Clusters of galaxies in Corona Borealis.

Small instruments will not show the spiral structure in galaxies as seen in photographs taken with large telescopes. Long-exposure photographs show that galaxies are made up of globular clusters, open clusters, variable stars and all the other stellar objects seen in our own Milky Way. It is likely too that planets exist in these galaxies in systems similar to our own solar system, but they lie at such great distance that they are far beyond reach of any present-day earth-bound telescopes.

Finding One's Way About the Sky and Nomenclature

A CASUAL inspection of the sky on a clear, moonless night shows the heavens strewn with stars which seemingly—at first glance—exist in numbers uncountable. However, with interest aroused, the observer will soon notice that the visible stars are not distributed uniformly over the sky; and if an attempt is made to count them, there are surprisingly fewer than one thought. On such a clear, moonless night any single observer may see up to about 3,000 stars at any one time. This may seem a great many, but when compared with the total number in the Milky Way and the rest contained in all the galaxies that form the visible Universe, it is but a drop in the ocean.

The realization that the number of visible stars, especially the brighter ones, is limited, and that they are not uniformly distributed about the sky, is actually the first step towards recognizing the star patterns and constellations. Quite a short period of observation will reveal that the stars, just as the Sun and Moon, rise in the east, climb up in the sky and sink again towards the western horizon. Observations extended over consecutive nights will show that the stars appear to make one complete circuit of the sky in about twenty-four hours. Observations will also show that the star sphere appears to be rotating round a 'pivot'— owing to the daily rotation of the Earth. Actually there are two such pivots: one in the northern and one in the southern hemisphere, called the north and south celestial poles respectively. The height, or altitude, these pivots make above the horizon depends on the latitude from which the observer is looking; this measured angle is the observer's real latitude and can be used for navigational purposes.

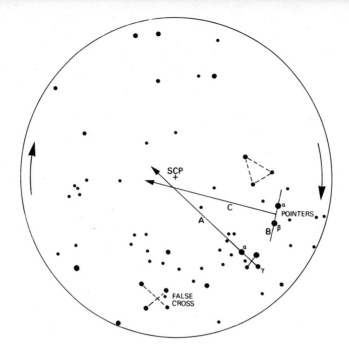

Fig. 9 *Locating the south celestial pole from Crux and Centaurus. (Fig. 10) using Cassiopeia to locate the north celestial pole if Ursa Major is below the horizon. Note horizon cut-offs for different latitudes.*

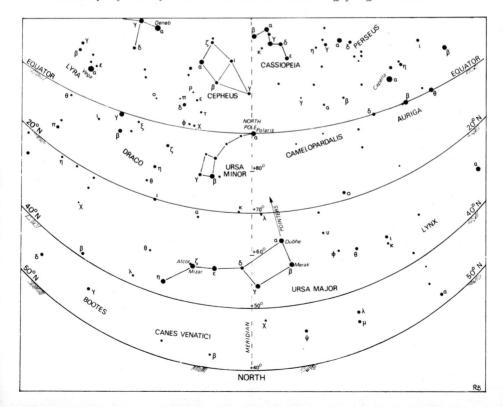

In the northern hemisphere the south celestial pole is invisible, since it is located below the observer's southern horizon; in the southern hemisphere it is the reverse situation, with the north celestial pole hidden below the northern horizon.

An observer in the northern hemisphere has a slight advantage over one in the southern, since round the north celestial pole are some very distinctive guide constellations. Very close to the northern pivot point is the 2nd-magnitude star Polaris (the Pole or North Star). Not far away from Polaris is one of the principal key constellations actually used to find Polaris. This is the constellation of Ursa Major (Latin for Great Bear). Since it is rotating about the north celestial pole, in common with adjacent constellations, it may be found at any position of the 'clock face', depending on the time of the day and the month of the year if we imagine Polaris to be the pivot point for the hour hand. (p. 5)

For observers in northern temperate latitudes (above latitude *c.* 40° N), the Great Bear never dips below the horizon. For those observers in latitudes less than *c.* 40° N, the constellation of Cassiopeia, forming the distinctive 'W' or 'M' (depending on its position on the 'clock face'), can be used to indicate Polaris when the Great Bear is below the horizon (*see* Fig. 10).

In the southern hemisphere there is no really bright star near the celestial pole to mark it out clearly and unambiguously. Nevertheless its approximate location can be found by using the bright stars in the constellation of Centaurus as southern pointers and in addition the stars of the Southern Cross can be used (*see* Fig. 9).

Observers in either hemisphere will soon note that any star or constellation whose distance from the celestial pole (or pivot) is less than the distance of the pivot point to the horizon (below the pole) can never set for the observer; or expressed another way these stars and constellations never disappear from view below the horizon. All such stars and constellations are called circumpolar; in the northern temperate latitudes the Great Bear is an example of such a constellation, and in the latitudes of South Africa, Australia and New Zealand the Southern Cross is another.

It will be recalled it was stated earlier that the star sphere appears to make a complete circuit once every twenty-four hours owing to the Earth's rotation. But if the star sphere rotated in exactly twenty-four hours, the same stars would rise at the same time night after night, and we would see the same constellations in the summer as we do in winter. Even the most casual of stargazers will soon see that this is not the case, and the winter stars and constellations are not the same as those of summer (except, of course, the circumpolar ones). The reason is that the stars do not make one daily circuit of the star sphere in exactly twenty-four hours—but in a period some four minutes shorter. Thus clock time is slower than star time, and even night-to-night observation extended over a week will reveal that the stars and constellations are gradually shifting position in relation to the exact time they pass a fixed object. The reason for this gradual shift is that the Earth is not only spinning on its axis (once in twenty-four hours), but it is also revolving round the Sun in a period of one year; this causes a steady change of the observer's viewpoint of the Sun and stars from minute to minute and from day to day. The four minutes' difference accumulated each day multiplied by the days in the year equals twenty-four hours, consequently in one year we arrive back at the starting point again.

Star Positions

Just as with terrestrial maps we can locate, without too much difficulty, the position of a city or large town simply by inspecting the map if we know the district or country in which it lies, so it is with a bright star if we know the constellation to which it belongs. But just as with an obscure village or geographical name we would need to consult a gazetteer to find its grid reference, or its latitude and longitude, the same principle applies to the fainter, more

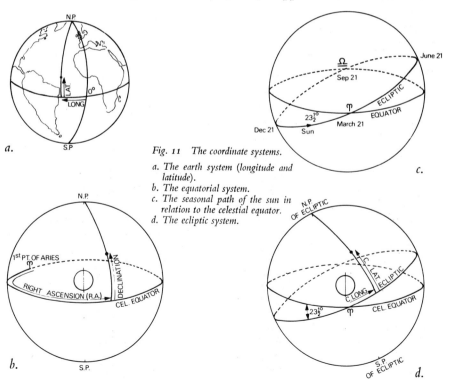

Fig. 11   The coordinate systems.

a. The earth system (longitude and latitude).
b. The equatorial system.
c. The seasonal path of the sun in relation to the celestial equator.
d. The ecliptic system.

obscure stars. However, instead of a grid reference, or latitude and longitude, we use coordinates known as Right Ascension and Declination—the exact analogues of longitude and latitude.

The celestial coordinates were invented in the dim and distant past as an imaginary fixed grid to measure against. Right Ascension differs from terrestrial longitude only in that it can be expressed in both angular measure, i.e. degrees (°), minutes (') seconds (") and also in time—hours, minutes and seconds. It is more usual to use the latter, since Right Ascension is also directly related to Sidereal Time (or star time). Time is more convenient for astronomers who are for ever having to take into account different kinds of time in their reckonings, the subject of which is outside the scope of our considerations here (*see* the author's *Astronomy in Colour*).

All coordinate systems require zero reference points. Terrestrial longitude is referred to the Greenwich meridian, and latitude to the Equator. If the Earth's axis was not inclined (at $23\frac{1}{2}°$), the apparent path followed by the Sun, Moon and planets, called the ecliptic, would coincide with the imaginary line known as the celestial equator. But since the Earth's axis is tilted $23\frac{1}{2}°$, the equator and the ecliptic are in separate planes (*see* Fig. 11c). Where these planes cross, are found the Spring and Autumn equinox points; or, in other words, they are the positions of the Sun about 21 March and 22 September each year. It was the ancient astronomers who hit upon the idea of using the location of the Spring Equinox as a zero point to measure Right Ascension, which is then carried round the celestial sphere in an eastern, or counterclockwise, direction until it comes back to zero again. Declination is always measured as a plus (+) or minus (−) angle, north and south respectively of the celestial equator (*see* Key Maps pp. 39–45 and Deep Sky Charts pp. 48–67).

In professional observatories, telescopes are equipped with special circles so that objects can be found by setting the correct Right Ascension and Declination gleaned from a catalogue. This is because large astronomical telescopes are housed in domes and have very small angular fields of view; and without the use of celestial coordinates, astronomers would waste an enormous amount of valuable observing time attempting to line up their telescopes by eye exactly on the object to be studied.

Now, although it is necessary for star and planet spotters to understand how celestial objects are referenced by coordinates, the method of giving Right Ascension (RA) and Declination (Dec) for each object is not employed in this book except in certain appendices (in the planet spotting tables (pp. 127–138) a slightly different but related coordinate method is used).

The stars and constellations are located directly by using the Key Star Maps and Charts provided. If the most distinctive ones are first identified in the sky, these can then be used as reference markers, and the fainter, less distinctive ones will fall into place like pieces in a jigsaw puzzle. Again, when employing binoculars to find a faint deep-sky object, a brighter near-by star pattern is first located; then when this is correctly identified in the sky, the fainter object can be swept up by applying the necessary offset. This direct method of star spotting leads to a much more intimate knowledge of the night sky than that gained by professional astronomers who are cut off from a view of the heavens by the telescope dome.

Precession and the Wandering Pole Stars

Over a period of *c.* 26,000 years the Earth completes an axial 'wobble' which causes the Right Ascension and Declination of stars and other 'fixed' celestial bodies to change continuously. This slow wobbling of the Earth's axis was discovered in *c.* 150 B.C., by the Greek Hipparchus who noted that the position of the stars he had begun to recatalogue did not match up with the positions given in an earlier catalogue.

The wobble of the Earth's axis is called precession and is referred to under its full title as *the precession of the equinoxes.* It brings about a slow displacement of the star sphere which causes the Sun to change its position where it crosses the Vernal (Spring) Equinox (zero point for Right Ascension) by an advancement westward of 50″ per annum, so that star coordinates need to be referred to a particular year. However, for ordinary star and planet spotting purposes this annual change has no significance (*see* also Constellation Boundaries p. 29).

Fig. 12   The circles show the path of the Earth's axis in each hemisphere over a period of about 26,000 years.

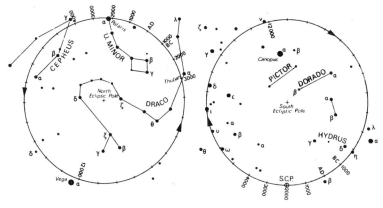

The cause of precession is due to the gravitational attraction of the Sun and the Moon tending to pull at the Earth's equatorial bulge. This action is opposed by the rotation of the Earth and results in an oscillation of the Earth's axis around *the pole of the ecliptic* (much as occurs in a spinning top) in a circle 47° in diameter in a period of *c.* 26,000 years. One important consequence is that over long time intervals it causes both pole stars to change. For example, in the northern hemisphere 12,000 years ago, Vega (α Lyrae) was the pole star; in *c.* 3000 B.C. it was Thuban (α Draconis). By *c.* A.D. 4000, Errai (γ Cephei) will have displaced α Ursae Minoris as the pole star (*see* Fig. 12 and pp. 29 and 83).

Star Nomenclature

The principal stars in each constellation are designated by letters of the Greek alphabet and by their Arabic names. Generally speaking only the brighter stars have Arabic names (*see* Star Name Index).

α	Alpha	ι	Iota	ρ	Rho
β	Beta	κ	Kappa	σ	Sigma
γ	Gamma	λ	Lambda	τ	Tau
δ	Delta	μ	Mu	u	Upsilon
ε	Epsilon	ν	Nu	φ	Phi
ζ	Zeta	ξ	Xi	χ	Chi
η	Eta	o	Omicron	ψ	Psi
θ	Theta	π	Pi	ω	Omega

Usually, but not always (*see* p. 73), the brightest star in each constellation is designated α, and the next brightest β and so on. When the Greek letters are exhausted for a particular constellation, Roman letters are used. Flamsteed (1646–1716), the first Astronomer Royal, introduced his own system of identifying stars by denoting them with the number in his catalogue (in order of their increasing Right Ascension). Later observers and organizations introduced designations of their own and introduced special nomenclatures for double stars, variable stars, clusters, nebulae, etc. (*see* below).

Owing to the various synonymous systems, a bright star may be identified in several ways: for example, Aldebaran (Arabic name), α (Alpha) Tauri (Bayer's method), 87 (Flamsteed's number), 1420 B.A.C. (British Association Catalogue number) and 8637 Ll (the number in the catalogue of the French astronomer Lalande).

Examples of Specialist Star Catalogues

Aitken's Double Star Catalogue (A.D.C.)
Astrographic Catalogue (A.Z.)
British Association Catalogue (B.A.C.)
Bonn Durchmusterung (B.D.)
Boss' General Catalogue (G.C.)
Burnham's General Catalogue of Double Stars (B.G.C.)
Lacaille's Catalogue of Southern Stars (Lac.)
Sir William Herschel's Catalogue (H)
Sir John Herschel's Catalogue (h)
Sir John Herschel's Catalogue of Sir William Herschel's Double Stars (Hh)
F. G. W. Struve's list (Σ)
Otto Struve's list ($O\Sigma$)
Pulkova Catalogue ($O\Sigma\Sigma$)
Contractions are shown in brackets.

Variable Star Nomenclature

Except for those stars with Greek designations, variable stars are designated by a Roman capital letter beginning with R through to Z and followed by the name of the constellation, e.g. R Andromedae (genitive case used). When more than nine variables were discovered in any one constellation, double letters were introduced, e.g. RR, RZ, etc. to ZZ. Later, with additional discoveries, more letter combinations had to be introduced, so it continued with AA, AZ, etc. In this method there are 325 combinations available. Nowadays, since faint variable stars are discovered in large numbers, any new variable found in a constellation which already has 334 variables is designated by an Arabic number only, preceded with a Roman capital V, e.g. V 515 Persei. One of the best known catalogues of variable stars is *Catalogue of Variable Stars* by the Soviet astronomers Kukarkin and Parengo.

Galaxies, Nebulae, Star Clusters and Other Celestial Objects are also catalogued in various ways. The brighter galaxies, nebulae and star clusters were first catalogued by the Frenchman Charles Messier in 1784, and his original list numbering 103 objects, M 1, M 2, etc., is still in current use. However, the discoveries of William Herschel and others soon increased the total number into many thousands. In 1888, the British astronomer Dreyer formulated the *New General Catalogue* (NGC). For example, the Great Nebula in Andromeda (p. 74) is M 31 *or* NGC 224. Later a supplementary Index Catalogue (IC. or I. followed by a number, i.e. I.2627) was published.

Star and Planet Brightness (Magnitudes)

The first inspection of the sky by a new observer reveals that the stars differ among themselves in apparent brightness. These differences depend on three factors: different star luminosities, different star sizes, and the fact that stars are located at varying distances from the Earth. It was the Greek astronomer Hipparchus who first adopted the idea to divide all the visible stars into six arbitrary grades of brightness. The very brightest were called 1st-magnitude stars and the next 2nd-magnitude and so on down to the 6th—which is approximately the faintest star that can be seen on a clear, moonless night with the naked eye.

This magnitude system was satisfactory until the invention of the telescope, but when it was extended to lower levels, it was found to be too pragmatic— particularly when observational astronomy began to make rapid advances in the nineteenth century. In about 1850 the system was first given a precise definition. At this time it was agreed to base magnitudes on a logarithmic scale whereby a 1st-magnitude star was 2·512 times brighter than a 2nd-magnitude star. Instead of guesswork, each magnitude was related to the next in a precise scale, thus the difference between five magnitudes corresponds *exactly* to a ratio 100 : 1.

In addition other alterations were necessary; some of Hipparchus's 1st-magnitude stars needed to be upgraded to include the concept of zero (o) and minus (−) magnitudes. Thus a star of magnitude o (zero) is 2·512 times *brighter* than a 1st-magnitude star, and a minus one (−1) magnitude star is 2·512 times brighter than a o-magnitude star. Even the ancient astronomers felt that whole magnitude steps were too crude to show precise differences of brightness between stars and therefore used fractions of a magnitude, e.g. one-and-one-third. Modern astronomers use a decimal system and represent stars to a tenth, a hundredth or even a thousandth of a magnitude, using an instrument called a photometer. Experienced visual observers are able to detect differences of one-tenth of a magnitude by using the eye alone.

The brightest star in the sky, Sirius (α CMa), is magnitude (mag) −1·4; the planet Venus at its most brilliant in the evening and morning skies is mag −4·4. The Moon is mag −12·7, and the Sun mag −26·7. The magnitude of the planets depends not on luminosity, for they all shine by reflected sunlight. As a consequence the brightness of a planet is determined by: (*a*) Its diameter.

(*b*) Its distance from the Sun and the Earth. (*c*) Its reflective power, or surface albedo. A planet such as Mars varies its apparent brightness considerably owing to its changing distance from the Earth during its revolution round the Sun.

To the limit of magnitude 6, some 3,000 stars are visible to the naked eye on any clear, moonless night. With 8 × 30 binoculars, stars of magnitude 9 are just visible and number about 200,000. The 200-in diameter Palomar telescope can reach magnitude 23. In the future, new telescopes, in conjunction with electronic image intensifiers, will be able to record stars of magnitude 30, and in numbers simply uncountable.

Constellation Boundaries

Until 1930, when the International Astronomical Union standardized the constellation boundaries, there was much confusion about the boundary lines separating the different constellations. In the old star atlases, produced by the first celestial cartographers (*see* Pl. 1 and Fig. 1) it is often doubtful to which constellation a particular star belongs. The very earliest star maps had no boundaries; these were introduced in 1801 by the German astronomer Bode, who drew between the mythical figures arbitrary lines without any thought of what the effect of long-term precession might have in displacing them (*see* p. 25).

After Bode, when other astronomers decided on their own boundary modifications, the situation became chaotic. The new boundaries decided by IAU run 'squarely' exactly along the direction of the celestial coordinates RA and Dec. These boundary lines, like the stars themselves, are subject to precessional movement, so that when a new star atlas or a set of charts is constructed, it is always quoted as belonging to a particular epoch, e.g. 1900. All the maps and charts in this book are based on epoch 1950 and are sufficiently accurate so that for the purposes intended they can be used long after the year 2000 without any adjustment.

Observing Aids

FOR simple star and planet recognition there is no better tool than the naked eye with its all-embracing wide-angle view of the heavens. However, although naked-eye star and planet spotting can provide endless satisfaction and pleasure, a pair of inexpensive binoculars or a small telescope greatly increases the range of objects that can be studied. Even a simple opera-glass—similar in principle to Galileo's first telescope—enables the stargazer to penetrate the normal visual limits and explore the regions totally unknown to man until the dawn of the seventeenth century.

Modern observational astronomy began a little over three centuries ago with the invention of the telescope in about 1608. When Galileo heard about it, he quickly built one for himself and applied it to a comprehensive study of the sky. The stars, although they still remained only scintillating points of light, were revealed to exist in innumerable numbers. However, the planets, or wanderers, which to the ancients were also points of light, were resolved into discs, and in the case of Jupiter, the four brighter attendant moons were easily seen.

Ideally, newcomers to star and planet spotting should resist the immediate temptation to observe with binoculars or telescopes until they have learnt to find their way about the sky with the naked eye. In this way a star and planet spotter will develop a familiarity with the heavens which will provide a foundation for subsequent deep-sky 'forays' with binoculars or a small telescope.

The principal advantage that optical assistance brings to observation is light grasp. The human eye with a diameter of only 5 mm (one-fifth of an inch) compares very unfavourably with the light collecting area of the objective lens of ordinary 8 × 30 prismatic binoculars which have an area over forty times greater.

A second advantage is what is termed resolving power. This is the ability to resolve, or separate, fine detail, especially with objects which are close together and which appear as single with the unassisted eye. This resolving power is expressed in seconds of arc and is based on an empirical formula first set down by an English clergyman-cum-amateur astronomer William R. Dawes in 1850—nowadays referred to as 'the Dawes limit'. Resolving power is of paramount importance when observing double stars and planetary detail. In the case of double stars a 1-in (2·54-cm) diameter telescope will theoretically resolve (or separate) two equal stars which are 4·5″ (4½ seconds of arc) apart.

In practice this ability is dependent on the quality of the optical surfaces and it also requires a minimum magnification, usually assumed to be about ×25 per inch of aperture.

Generally speaking, since opera glasses and prismatic binoculars are held in the hand, and otherwise unsupported, they have relatively low magnifications. This is because even the smallest hand shake or tremor is also magnified proportionally, and with magnifications greater than about ×8, using hand-held binoculars for astronomical viewing is difficult. But other factors also enter the choice of binocular specification. One important factor concerns the field of view, since generally the *greater* the magnifying power employed, the *smaller* is the field of view, and in the case of terrestrial viewing the less brilliant the object will appear when large magnifications are used. This is because the light collected by the objective lens is constant and has to be spread over a larger area.

The older type of field and opera glass, nowadays found in antique shops and some theatres, generally employ low magnifications extending from about ×2 to ×6. These instruments operate on the principle of the Galilean optical system which has now been almost completely superseded by the prismatic optical system used in modern binoculars. However, for astronomical purposes, these older instruments are not to be despised, for they provide some glorious views of star fields and clusters—particularly those in the richer parts of the Milky Way.

Modern prismatic binoculars have a more complex system and can be designed to give a wide field of view in combination with higher magnifications

Fig. 13   Typical binoculars and field glasses useful for star and planet spotting.

Figs. 14 and 15 A selection of binoculars, with a 5 cm (2 in) telescope and comet-hunting 25 × 105 binoculars (right). See p. 149 for key to binoculars and accessories.

than the Galilean type. Typical of contemporary binoculars (used by the author) are 8 × 30s which translated means: magnification eight times, objective lens (the front one) 30 mm ($1\frac{3}{16}$ in.) in diameter. This particular model gives a field of view of $8\frac{1}{2}°$; in some models the field of view is expressed in so many yards (or metres) per thousand fee (or metres). Another model is 7 × 35 which provides a field of view of $11\frac{1}{2}°$. Occasionally one finds binoculars with fields of view extending to 13°, but usually such instruments are relatively expensive and even then give blurred images at the outer edge of the field of view so that the extra-wide angle advantage is lost.

Most prismatics have coated lenses which increase the light transmitting power by cutting down on light lost by reflection. It can lead, in identical models, one coated and one uncoated, to differences of one or more star magnitudes—so it can be seen that it is highly advantageous to have fully coated optics for the observations of faint deep-sky objects near the borderline of visibility.

Many low-priced binoculars suffer from a defect known as chromatic aberration—shown as a colourful display of rainbow tints when a bright object is viewed—caused by mismatched optical components. Now, although this effect is a nuisance, for simple astronomical observations these inexpensive binoculars are still very useful and are certainly better than none at all if the observer's financial resources are limited. All the early refracting telescopes suffered from this chromatic defect, but it did not prevent their users from making significant discoveries.

Binoculars have an advantage not possessed by telescopes in that by viewing with both eyes, the eyes are more relaxed, and it means that binoculars can be used for longer observing spells without straining the eyes and the muscles surrounding them.

When contemplating a new binocular purchase for deep-sky viewing, the universal 8 × 30 model may be regarded as the median type. There are hundreds of brands and varieties on the world market, but preference should be given to a pair with a wide-angle view: say 450 feet at 1,000 yards, providing at least 7·5° true field or expressed another way, one-and-a-half times the distance between the Pointer Stars in the Great Bear. If the pocket can be stretched a little further, it is well worth investing in a pair of extra-wide angle 7 × 35s: say 500–550 feet at 1,000 yards, or a true field of *c.* 11° plus. Both these types of binoculars can also be used for ordinary terrestrial purposes.

Although the heavy, hand-held binoculars of the 7 × 50 'night glass' type collect more light, they can only be used effectively in truly coal-black skies. In towns or semi-rural environments they transmit too much of the bright, scattered background light in the sky so that no advantage is gained (except in resolution) over the smaller, much handier 8 × 30s and 7 × 35s—which are much lighter in weight and therefore less tiring to hold.

The large ex-military, mounted reconnaissance binoculars of the 10 × 80 or 25 × 105 varieties (for author's binoculars *see* Figs. 14 and 15) are more difficult to come by these days, but they can still be found advertised occasionally in astronomical magazines, and periodicals which specialize in advertising second-hand optical goods.

The naked-eye or binocular observer will find a reclining garden chair especially convenient for gazing at the sky overhead. A garden chair with arms provides an ideal elbow rest to steady hand-held binoculars, and steadiness is *essential* when operating at the optical limit of a pair of binoculars. An alternative method of steadying binoculars is to mount them on a small camera tripod (set on a table) by means of an inexpensive binocular adapter (Fig. 14)

Fig. 16   A garden chair is ideal for relaxed star and planet spotting.

which can be readily purchased from many optical stores. Using a tripod is very convenient when working with star charts or books, for once the right field is located, the binoculars can be left in position and the hands remain free to consult a reference, to make a drawing, or write notes. For working at the limit of binocular vision a tripod mounting, or its equivalent, is absolutely essential to obtain the best results.

Advice and hints

In star and planet spotting, as in everything else, practice makes perfect. Many beginners bitten by the bug of observational astronomy rush outdoors and come back disappointed with their first view of the skies. Some consider they have been let down by descriptions of objects and magnificent photographs in books which, to say the least, exaggerate what can be seen with the naked eye or small instruments. There are several reasons for this disappointment. A principal reason is that many beginners go outdoors armed with a handbook and expect to see the Andromeda Nebula through binoculars (or even in a large size telescope) exactly as it is depicted in the long-exposure photographs taken by some of the world's finest and largest telescopes.

What the observer actually sees when he looks through his binoculars or telescope at a galaxy is usually a faint, misty patch of light, sometimes at the limit of visibility; if he is a newcomer, he may not see anything at all! But part of the trouble also stems from the beginner's unawareness of the importance of what is known as 'dark adaptation'. He will rush outdoors from an environment that has been flooded with bright electric lighting and plunge into inky blackness. Now the pupil of the eye requires time to dilate, and this interval of time varies considerably with different people. Some appear to adapt within a few minutes, while others may require upwards of fifteen minutes to half an hour. Actual adaptation begins fairly rapidly and continues to improve slowly over a long period outdoors. Observers who watch and sweep for comets are well aware of the slow process of dark adaptation. At the end of an hour-long spell of observation, when 'normal' dark adaptation has been achieved, large, faint objects are much more readily seen than shortly after first starting. Nebulae and star clusters which were missed completely on the first sweeps are as plain as pike staffs an hour or so later. Nevertheless, the casual star and planet spotter and deep-sky observer need not worry overmuch about spending *long* periods under a darkened sky in order to see the brighter stars, but it is recommended that he spends at least five minutes in the darkened outdoor environment before attempting simple star and constellation recognition.

For the star and planet spotter who becomes a really keen deep-sky observer, full dark adaptation is absolutely essential, and it must be remembered that all extraneous light must be kept to an absolute minimum. When the charts or text in this book have to be consulted outdoors, use a dim red-tinted light. Red light is best since it does not materially affect night vision. Illumination can be in form of an ordinary flash lamp or torch with the lens covered with red-tinted paper or cloth—or a spectacle-type head torch which leaves the hands free (*see* Fig. 14).

Harking back for a moment to the problem of initial disappointment experienced by some stargazers, it is my *own* experience that 'natural' views of faint nebulae and the scintillating frosty light of star clusters are far more aesthetically satisfying than the over-exposed 'blobs' of light shown in unrealistic photographs. Photographs like those shown in this book have their place in stimulating interest in amateur star spotters. But nothing can match up to the experience of observing through binoculars or a small telescope under the canopy of a cold, black winter's night when the stars are shimmering through the atmosphere in animated fashion, sometimes inducing an almost hypnotic effect on the eyes. No photograph can capture the myriad animated points of light that emerge from globular clusters such as the ones in Hercules and Centaurus; and no photograph can convey the gorgeously rich, ruby-red tint of stars like the Garnet Star in Cepheus. By contrast, if the observer prefers warm weather, there are few equally satisfying and relaxing experiences than to gaze into the soft, azure-blue darkness of a summer night sky from the comfort of a deck-chair and watch the stars in silent procession flit inexorably across the heavens. . . .

Apart from making full use of dark adaptation, there is another trick which can be utilized to enable the observer to detect faint objects. This is called averted vision. The centre part of the eye pupil is surprisingly less sensitive to light than the outer edge, so that if one glances sideways (averted), a faint patch or point of light at the extreme limit of vision can often be detected when it otherwise may escape notice. This trick can be used for sweeping up faint nebulae, clusters and comets.

When observing outdoors, the creature comforts of the body must not be neglected. It is well to bear in mind that two of the worst enemies of star and planet spotters are cold feet and cold hands. Men particularly should be warned to ensure that their wives or girlfriends are suitably clothed before enticing them into the great outdoors on a winter's night to share their enthusiasm of looking at stars and planets. If an observer contemplates to spend long periods outdoors in the cold months of the year, as may occur with an all-night meteor watch or marathon comet sweep, it is best to resort to some kind of insulated mountaineering clothing. These days quilted jackets and trousers are relatively inexpensive, and such clothes will keep out many degrees of frost even when reclined in a garden chair for several hours. If standing, another dodge is to keep the feet resting on an insulated board or just a square of timber. *Never* stand directly on a concrete or stone surface for long periods, since this will result in all the body-heat being conducted away. Keep warm drinks to a minimum. Although they do give a psychological uplift, their heating benefits at best are only transitory, and frequent visits to the 'loo' will not endear a budding star and planet spotter to the rest of the sleeping household—especially in the small hours of the morning.

Do's and Don'ts

(1) *Don't* ever look at the Sun directly with the naked eye, binoculars or telescopes as this can lead to permanent eye damage.

(2) *Do* remember to allow time for the eye to adapt to the darkness when going outdoors to spot stars and planets.

(3) *Don't* ever use an old rag to clean the lenses of binoculars or telescopes, use a chamois leather or an old, clean, soft cotton handkerchief; beware of patent spectacle cleaners which remove the high transmission coating from modern optics.

(4) *Don't* bore the rest of your family and friends with your initial enthusiasm at recognizing a constellation or identifying a planet: wean them to star and planet spotting slowly, this way you will win more converts.

(5) *Don't* brag about your own abilities to see faint objects to others whose eyesight is not as good as yours. When you have made a discovery of a nova or a new comet, with which your name will be associated for all time, you won't need to boast!

(6) *Do* expect to enjoy star and planet spotting. Seek out and join your local astronomical group (your local library may help in finding the address of their secretary) or contact more experienced stargazers in your district. However, *don't* expect more experienced amateurs to teach you star and planet spotting; they will be busy making their own observations, and after all you've bought (or borrowed) this book to teach yourself.

A beginner to variable star observation is recommended to make a start by following, with the naked eye, the light variations of Algol—called 'the Demon Star' by the Arabs. This is a convenient star to all observers whether they live in the northern hemisphere, in equatorial regions, or in the southern hemisphere.

Algol is an eclipsing binary variable, whose light variations are caused by a 'dark' companion periodically cutting off or eclipsing the brighter star as they both revolve round a common centre of gravity. This happens every sixty-nine hours, but the eclipse period occurs over a much shorter time.

Note that ordinarily Algol (β Per) will be slightly fainter than α Per, while the stars γ, δ, ϵ and ζ Per (p. 81) will be fainter than Algol. Two other stars close by, α and β Ari (p. 85), will ordinarily and respectively be brighter and fainter than Algol. Not far away are α and β (Tri) (see p. 104), which can be used as companion stars when the brightness of Algol has begun to fade.

Algol is now such a well-known star that an ephemeris (or a table of predictions) has been drawn up to indicate the exact times when light variations take place. These predictions can be found in several year books, almanacs and the topical monthly notes about stars in newspapers and magazines. However, it is much more interesting for the beginner to discover the times for himself by making observations over several nights.

When observations show that fading has begun (by comparing Algol with the companion stars named above) estimates of brightness should be noted along with two stars: one brighter and one fainter.

An observation may be as follows: Time 1977, August 1d 10h 15m, a 2/5 V 3/5 b. Translated this means that in 1977 on 1 August at 10.15 Universal Time (U.T.), Algol, denoted by 'V', was two-fifths of the interval *fainter* than the comparison star 'a' and three-fifths of the interval *brighter* than the comparison star 'b'. Some simple arithmetic (after substituting the magnitudes of 'a' and 'b') will give Algol's actual magnitude—expressed to the nearest tenth ($0 \cdot 1$) of a mag. Once variations have been noted, the observations should be repeated at half-hourly intervals to show how the brightness fluctuates with time (see Fig. 40).

Because of an insufficient period of darkness, it is unlikely that the observer will catch the whole light curve, since the decline and recovery takes Algol nine hours. The light diminishes for four-and-a-half hours, remains constant for a few minutes, then gradually increases again for another period of four-and-a-half hours. Even if the observer has only a very limited time for nightly perusal of the heavens, a methodical night-to-night inspection of Algol will one day catch 'the Demon Star' at the dim period of mid-eclipse.

A similar technique is adopted for binocular and telescopic variables. Most observers these days prefer—with experience gained—to work directly in magnitude units of one tenth (0·1), and some observers acquire the skill to recognize differences of 0·1 magnitude between comparison stars and the variables. Many observers estimate the brightness of the fainter optical variables by estimating the brightness of their out-of-focus (extrafocal) images. To do this the stars are purposely put out of focus so that they appear as homogeneous planetary-like discs of light. It is usually easier to carry the visual 'memory' of an extrafocal image out of the variable's field of view if another comparison star is not available near by, as often happens when observing a nova, or new star. This method is utilized for estimating the brightness of comets which are diffuse objects. It requires some experience, but it is the most accurate method available to visual observers. Estimates of bright comets by amateurs using this technique are often more reliable guides to cometary magnitudes than those given by professional astronomers. Indeed this is one of the fields in which amateurs can still perform original and important scientific research to supplement that done by full-time professional astronomers.

When choosing comparison stars to make estimates of a variable, it is best to choose stars, whenever possible, of the same spectral colour as the variable. Colour differences can lead to large errors, for the human eye is particularly sensitive to the light of blue and blue-white stars, but not to orange-red or red stars.

Key Star Maps

Note that the following key maps provide information when any particular star or constellation is visible to an observer *anywhere in the world*.

The calendar months printed at the bottom of the maps (or round the edge of the circle on the circumpolar maps) show the time of year when the constellations located immediately above the month are at their highest point on the observer's meridian (the true north-south line passing through the observer) at 9 p.m. (2100 hours) local time. When an observer wishes to make an observation before or after this time, remember that for each hour of clock time the star sphere is displaced one hour of Right Ascension, or 15° angular measure (i.e. 24 hours = 360°). However, to help the observer making this adjustment himself, the table below indicates approximately when any meridian will be due south, at various times of the year. Thus any star or star group on the meridian at 9 p.m. (2100 hrs) local time on 1 January will be approximately in the same position at 7 p.m. (1900 hrs) on 1 February; 11 p.m. (2300 hrs) on 1 December; 1 a.m. (0001 hrs) on 1 November; 3 a.m. (0003 hrs) on 1 October; 5 a.m. (0005 hrs) on 1 September.

The meridian due south at 9 p.m. (2100 hrs) on any given night in	Will be due south on the same night of the undermentioned months at				
	7 p.m. (1900 hrs)	11 p.m. (2300 hrs)	1 a.m. (0001 hrs)	3 a.m. (0003 hrs)	5 a.m. (0005 hrs)
January	Feb.	Dec.	Nov.	Oct.	Sept.
February	Mar.	Jan.	Dec.	Nov.	Oct.
March	April	Feb.	Jan.	Dec.	Nov.
April	May	Mar.	Feb.	Jan.	Dec.
May	June	April	Mar.	Feb.	Jan.
June	July	May	April	Mar.	Feb.
July	Aug.	June	May	April	Mar.
August	Sept.	July	June	May	April
September	Oct.	Aug.	July	June	May
October	Nov.	Sept.	Aug.	July	June
November	Dec.	Oct.	Sept.	Aug.	July
December	Jan.	Nov.	Oct.	Sept.	Aug.

The intermediate hours required can easily be reckoned from the above.

It will be noted that the key star maps consist of Northern Circumpolar Stars, Equatorial Stars and Southern Circumpolar Stars. Which stars are circumpolar (or always above the star spotter's horizon), and what equatorial stars can be seen will depend on the latitude from where observations are made and also on the time of night and the month of the year. For observers who wish to find (and perhaps mark *lightly* in pencil) the limit of star and constellation visibility for their own latitude, apply the following simple method.

Equatorial Key Maps: Take the latitude away from 90° and the remainder is the *southern* or *northern* declination limit.

Example: *northern hemisphere*, observer located at 51° North latitude. 90° minus
51° = 39° minus (−) declination limit.

Example: *southern hemisphere*, observer located at 40° South latitude. 90° minus
40° = 50° plus (+) declination limit.

Note: unlike terrestrial latitude which is measured north or south of the Equator, *declination* is measured from the *celestial equator* plus (+) in the northern celestial hemisphere and minus (−) in the southern celestial hemisphere.

Circumpolar Key Maps: To determine what stars and constellations are circumpolar for a particular latitude, take the latitude away from 90°.

Example: Observer located at 51° North latitude 90° minus 51° = 39°.

Thus at this northern latitude all stars and constellations in the northern celestial hemisphere with declinations greater than +39° will be circumpolar (or always above the observer's horizon).

Example: observer located at 51° South latitude 90° minus 51° = −39° (remember
minus (−) because of southern hemisphere).

Thus at this southern latitude all stars and constellations in the southern celestial hemisphere with declinations greater than −39° will be circumpolar.

Finding the Constellations

For star spotters making first attempts at star and constellation recognition it is recommended that a start is made with the circumpolar stars. Once the observer has located and recognized key circumpolar constellations or prominent objects—say Ursa Major (the Great Bear) and Cassiopeia in the northern hemisphere and Crux and the Magellanic Clouds (Nubecula Major and Nubecula Minor) in the southern hemisphere—by reference to the Key Maps the rest of the circumpolar and equatorial constellations will quickly fall into place like pieces in a jigsaw puzzle. For this purpose one can also use the deep-sky constellation charts pp. 46–67.

It will be seen, of course, that the nearer an observer is located to the Equator, the fewer will be the stars and constellations which are circumpolar, and exactly on the Equator itself *none* will be circumpolar; but some of the distinctive northern or southern key constellations will still be visible *above* the pole in both hemispheres (which ones depending on the time of night and the month).

A star spotter must bear in mind that because of haziness near the horizon, he will not see stars (except in unusual atmospheric conditions) until they have risen a few degrees above the horizon.

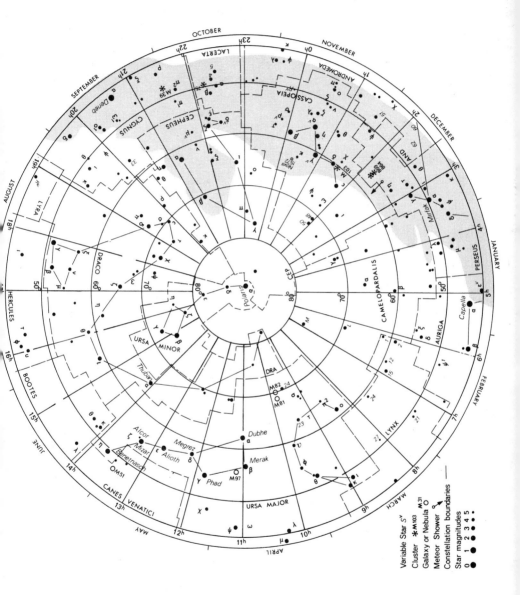

Variable Star S^v
Cluster ✻M103 M31
Galaxy or Nebula ○
Meteor Shower ✦
Constellation boundaries ——
Star magnitudes
0 1 2 3 4 5
● ● ● ● • •

Fig. 18 Equatorial Stars (RA 0h to 8h).

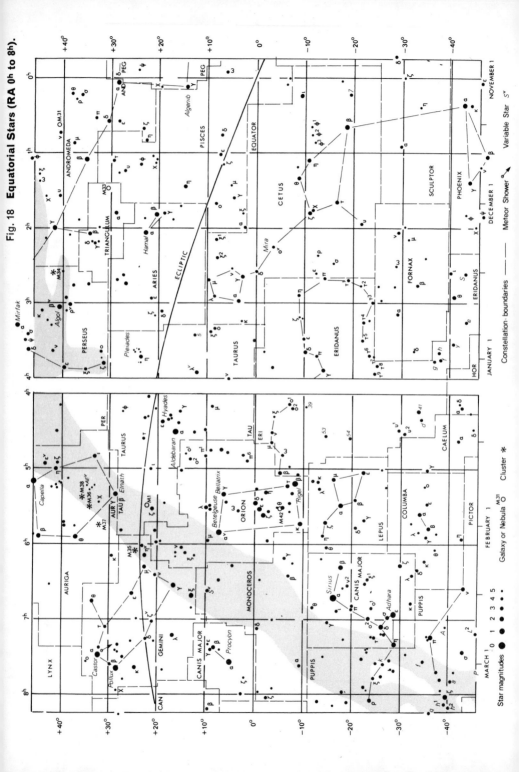

42

Fig. 19 Equatorial Stars (RA 8ʰ to 16ʰ).

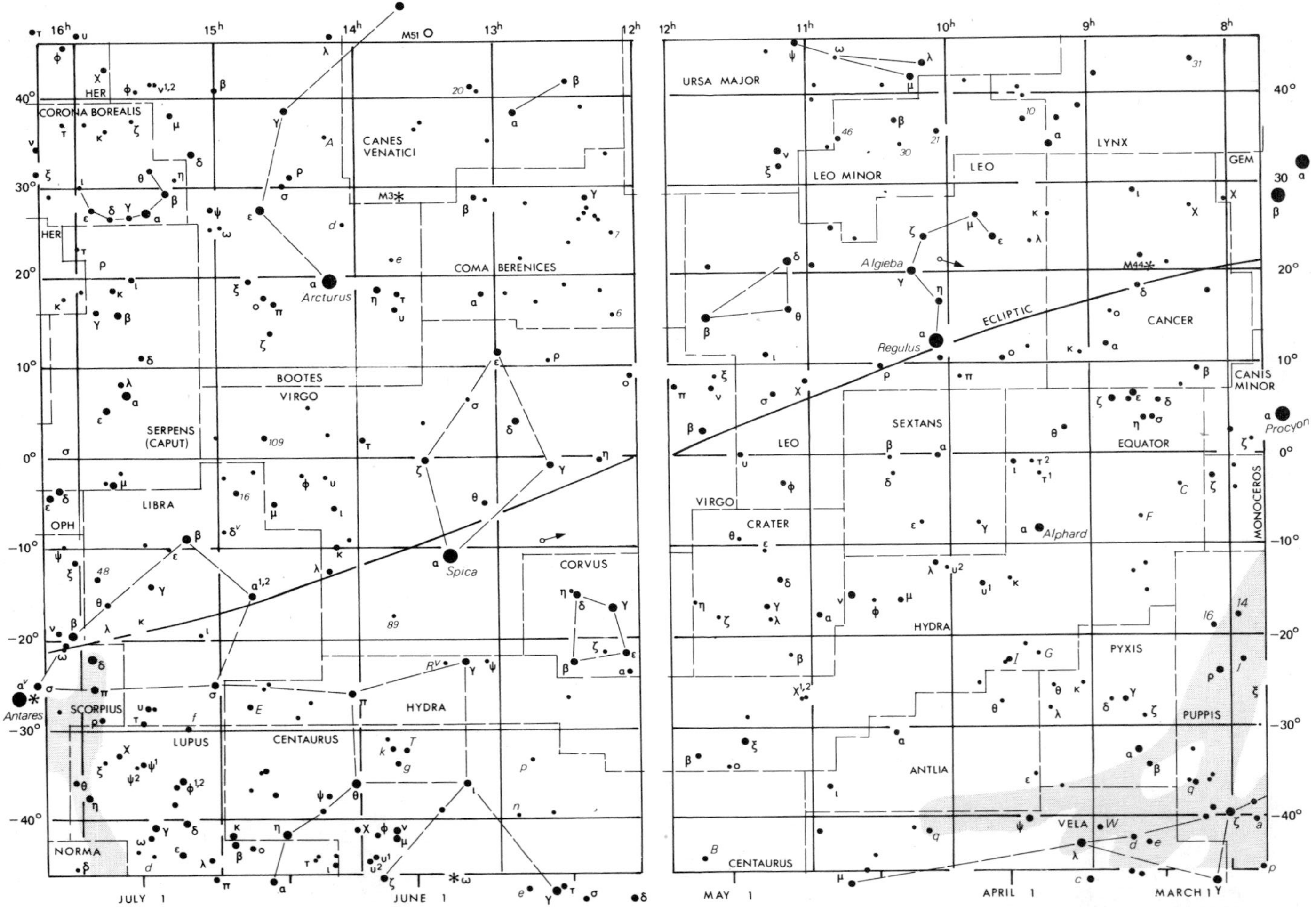

Fig. 20 **Equatorial Stars (RA 16h to 0h).**

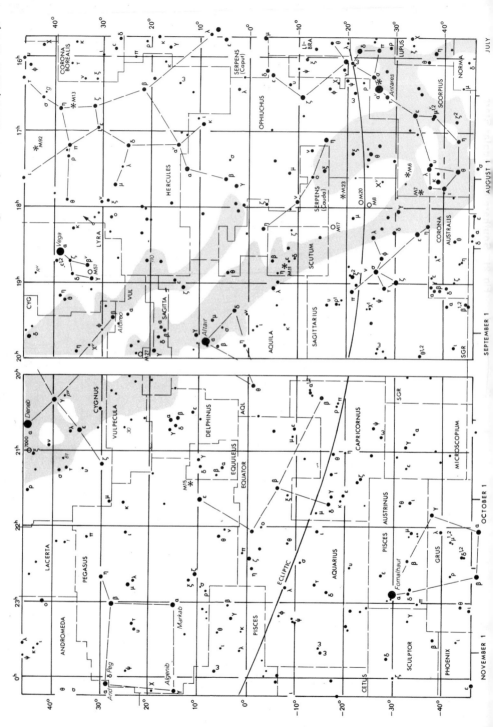

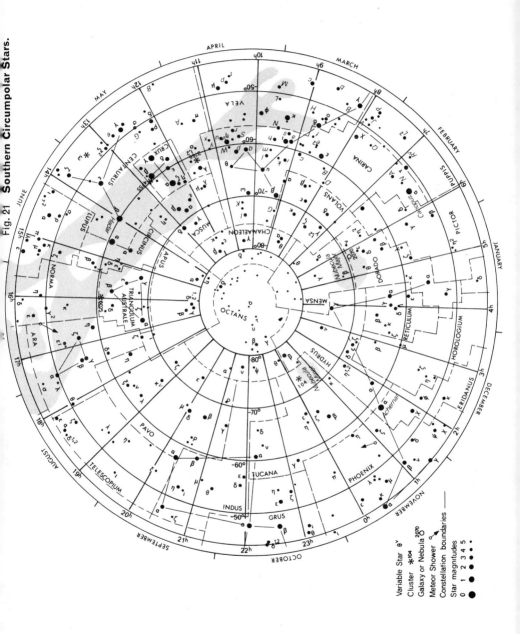

Fig. 21 Southern Circumpolar Stars.

Variable Star θ^v
Cluster ✳¹⁰⁴
Galaxy or Nebula 2070
Meteor Shower
Constellation boundaries ———
Star magnitudes
0 1 2 3 4 5

45

The Constellations and Deep-Sky Charts

THE following constellation descriptions and deep-sky charts cover the entire area of northern, equatorial and southern skies and are arranged in the following method:

Constellations

Name of constellation, followed by its recognized abbreviation (abbreviations only are used on the deep-sky charts).

The name of the mythological person, animal or object to which the constellation is traditionally referred.

A concise description about its location in relation to adjoining constellations or prominent stars and its particular characteristics including when it was formed, and by whom.

A short summary of the classical mythological legend associated with it.

The brightest stars in each constellation are named by their Greek designations and Arabic or other names, along with the brightness (magnitudes) and colours (*see* also p. 28 and abbreviations and conventions below).

Interesting objects are selected from the accompanying deep-sky charts suitable for observers using the naked eye, binoculars and small telescopes. Also included are references to important meteor showers associated with each constellation (*see* also p. 124 and abbreviations and conventions below).

Abbreviations and Conventions

star colours

These are described—in decreasing order of temperature—as greenish, blue, blue-white, white, yellowish-white, yellow, orange-yellow, orange-red, red (*see* also p. 13).

dia (or size)

Refers to the apparent angular diameter as seen by the observer and is measured in degrees (°), minutes (′) and seconds (″).

dist

In double, binary and multiple stars, 'dist' refers to the angular separation between component stars expressed in minutes (′) and seconds (″) of arc. Note that in double (binary) star descriptions the position angle of the fainter star to the brighter star (given in many catalogues) is not quoted as this information may be confusing or misleading and is not strictly necessary for making identifications.

mag

Stands for the magnitude, or brightness, of an object (see p. 28 for definition). The ability to see faint objects, or the limiting magnitude, depends on several factors but principally on the aperture of the binoculars or telescope. The larger the diameter of the objective lens (or mirror in a reflecting telescope) the fainter are stars that can be seen. Also the ability to resolve, or divide, double stars depends on the aperture, and the table (set out below) indicates the approximate performance the observer may expect with different sized telescopes. It must be remembered, however, that inferior instruments and inferior sky conditions may lead to much lower performances. Likewise, superior instruments and exceptional sky conditions will allow a slightly better performance. Note that with average quality low-power binoculars in the range ×6 to ×12 the magnification employed is generally insufficient to divide double stars with less than 1·5′ separation.

Diameter of Object Glass or Mirror	Naked eye	1-in	2-in	3-in	4-in	6-in	8-in	12-in
Closest Stars split	3′	4″·56	2″·28	1″·52	1″·14	0″·76	0″·57	0″·38
Magnitude Limit (approx.)	6	9·0	10·5	11·4	12·0	12·9	13·5	14·4

The limiting magnitudes of nebulae, galaxies and star clusters, apart from the considerations above, are also highly dependent on their angular size, sky transparency, and the amount of scattered sky light present in the observer's neighbourhood. Generally speaking their limiting magnitude is two magnitudes *brighter* than for stars, e.g. a 5-cm (2-in) telescope can show mag 10·5 stars but usually only mag 8·5 nebulae, etc. However, when the atmosphere is very transparent, for example, after rain, their threshold magnitudes often approach those of stars. Another important factor is that low magnification often accentuates a brighter sky background so that low-power wide-angle binoculars do not realize their theoretical aperture capabilities as indicated in the table above.

meteor showers

The radiant of the more active meteor showers is depicted on the deep-sky charts with an asterisk (★). Meteor showers are often referred to by the proximity of the radiant to an adjacent star, e.g. ζ Draconids.

numbering and lettering nomenclature

For the full explanation of methods used for stars, galaxies, star clusters and nebulae see pp. 26–28. Briefly, galaxies, nebulae and clusters are given their Messier Catalogue number (e.g. M 31) or the New General Catalogue number (e.g. NGC 1420) or the

continued on p. **73**

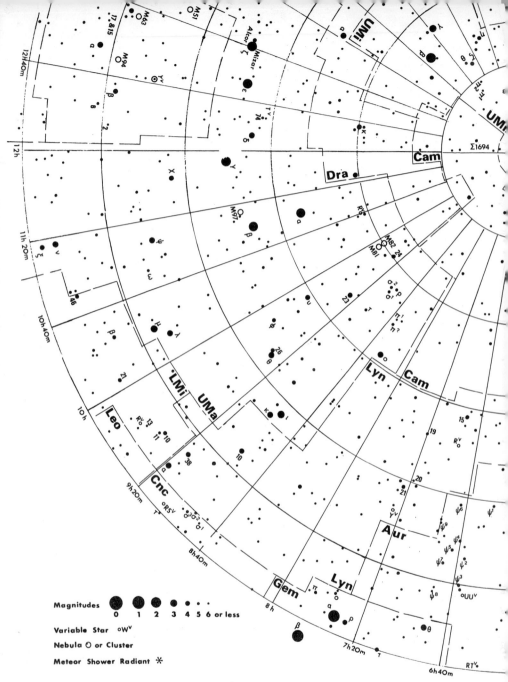

Magnitudes ● ● ● ● • • ·
0 1 2 3 4 5 6 or less

Variable Star ○W^v

Nebula ○ or Cluster

Meteor Shower Radiant ✳

Fig. 22   Northern Stars (RA 23ʰ 20ᵐ to 12ʰ 40ᵐ).

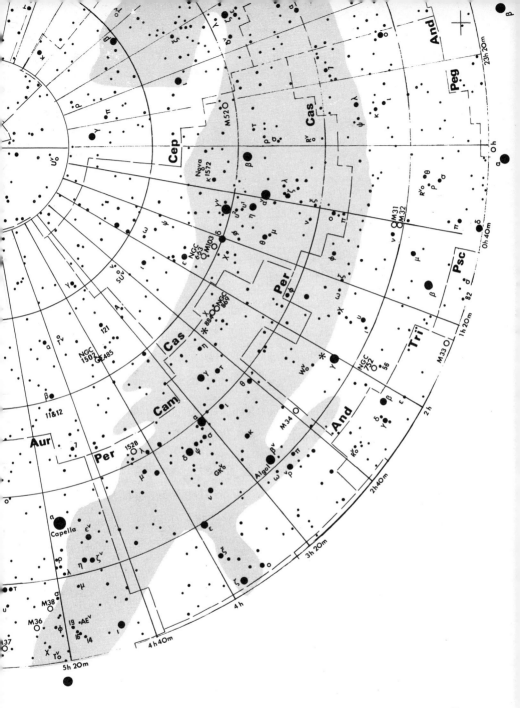

49

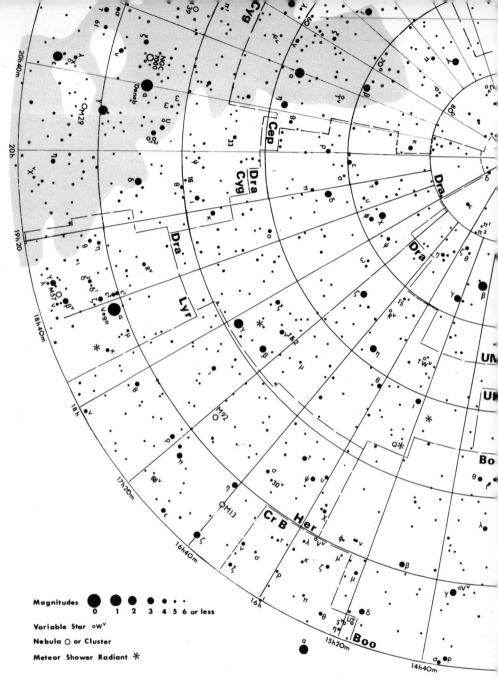

Magnitudes ● ● ● ● · ·
            0 1 2 3 4 5 6 or less

Variable Star oW^V

Nebula ○ or Cluster

Meteor Shower Radiant ✳

Fig. 23 Northern Stars (RA 7^h 20^m to 20^h 40^m).

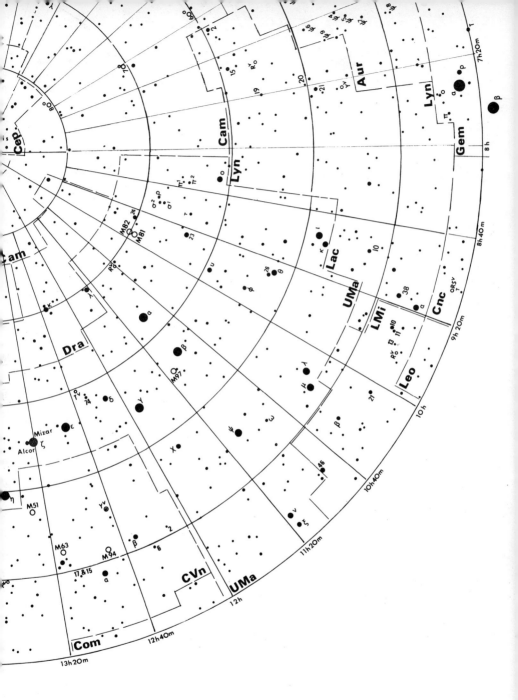

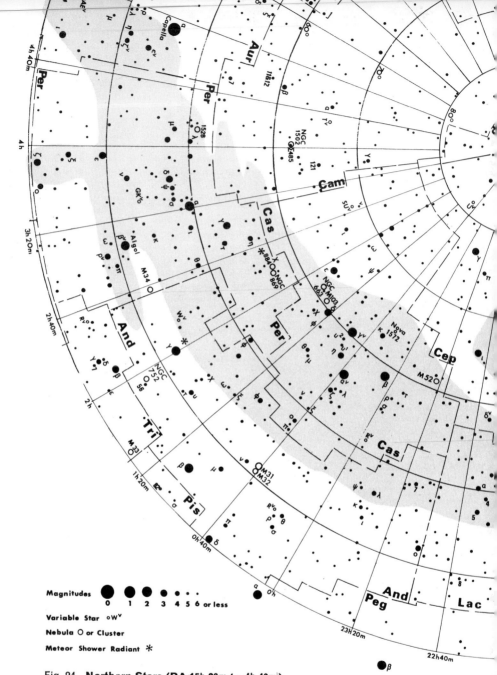

Magnitudes ● ● ● ● ● · · ·
0   1   2   3   4 5 6 or less

Variable Star ○Wᵛ

Nebula ○ or Cluster

Meteor Shower Radiant ✳

Fig. 24   **Northern Stars (RA 15ʰ 20ᵐ to 4ʰ 40ᵐ).**

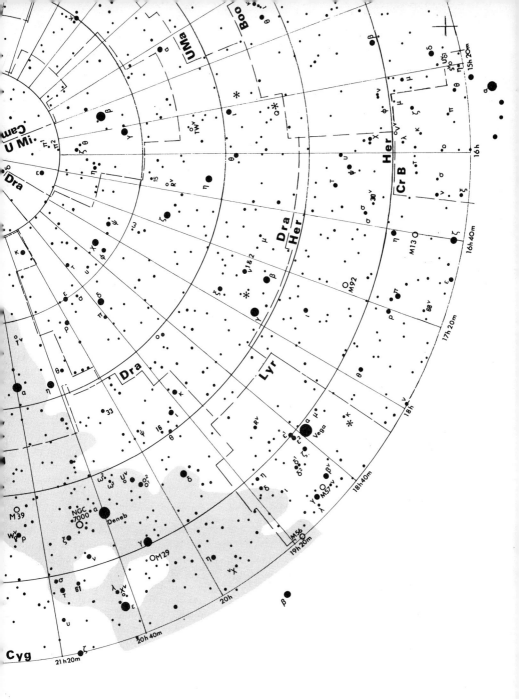

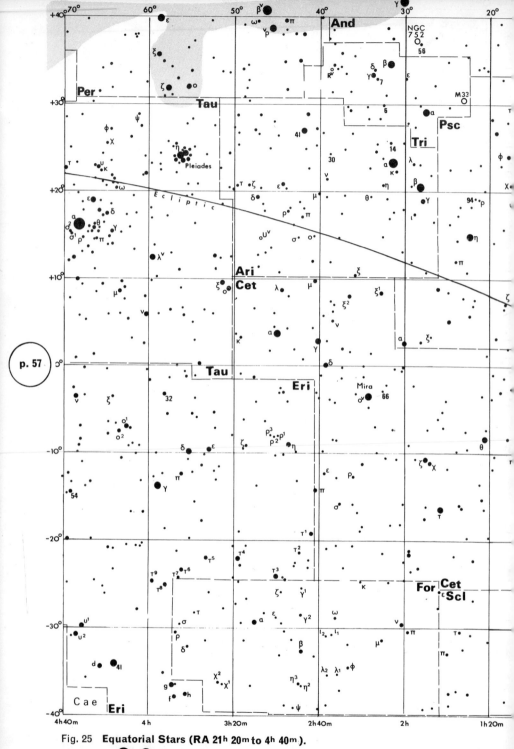

Fig. 25 **Equatorial Stars (RA 21ʰ 20ᵐ to 4ʰ 40ᵐ).**

Magnitudes ● ● ● ● ● · ·   Variable Star ○Wᵛ   Nebula ○ or Cluster
           0 1 2 3 4 5 6 or less

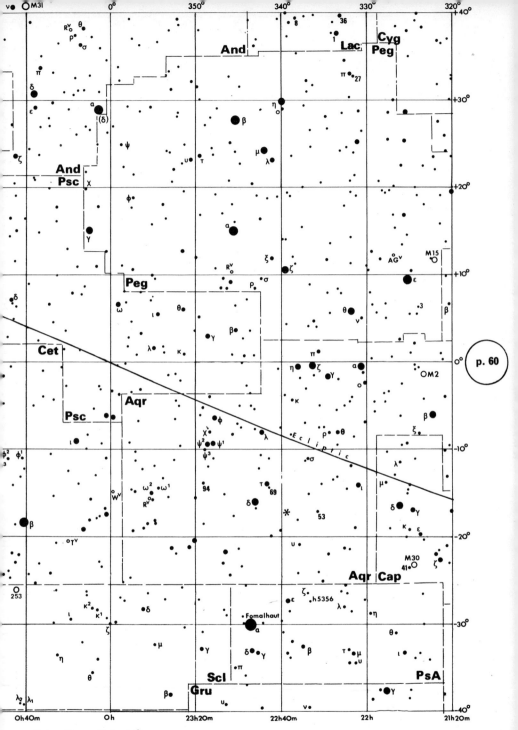

Meteor Shower Radiant ✳

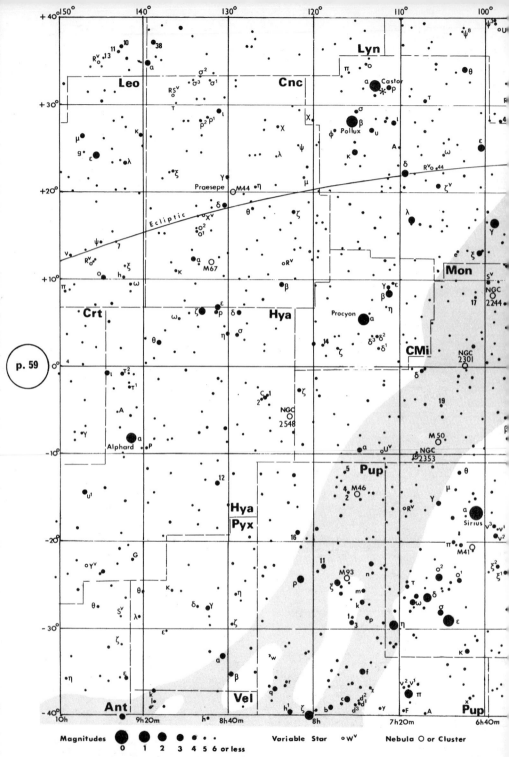

Fig. 26 Equatorial Stars (RA 2ʰ 40ᵐ to 10ʰ).

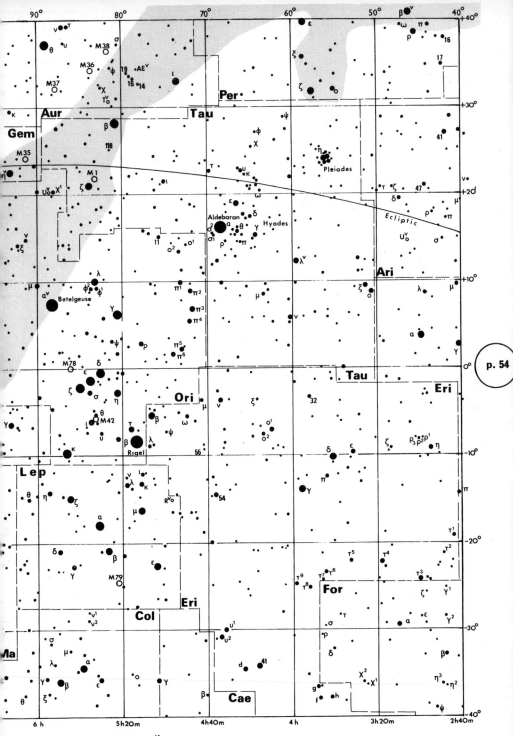

Meteor Shower Radiant ✳

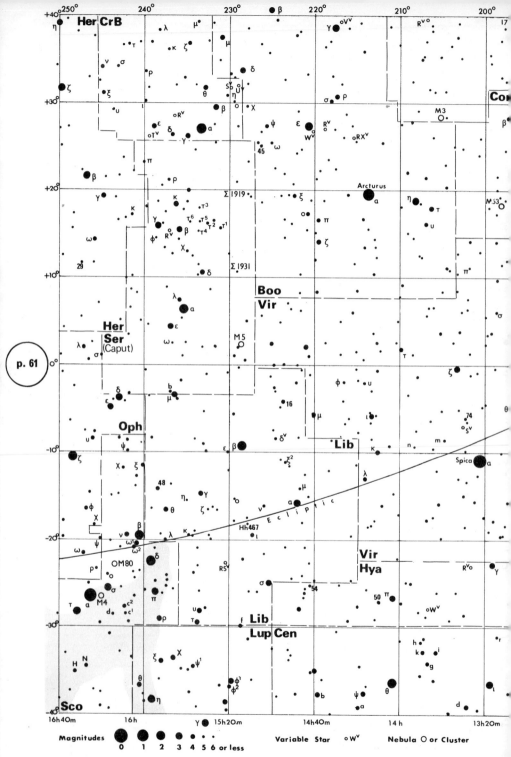

Fig. 27 Equatorial Stars (RA 9h 20m to 16h 40m).

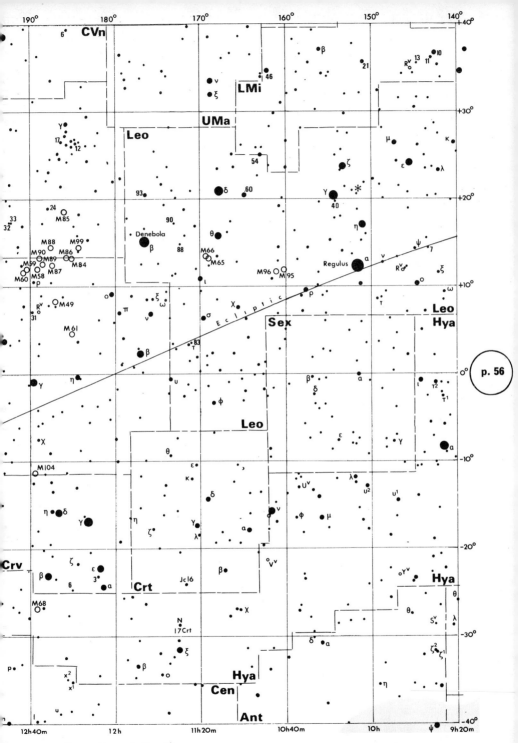

Meteor Shower Radiant ✳

p. 56

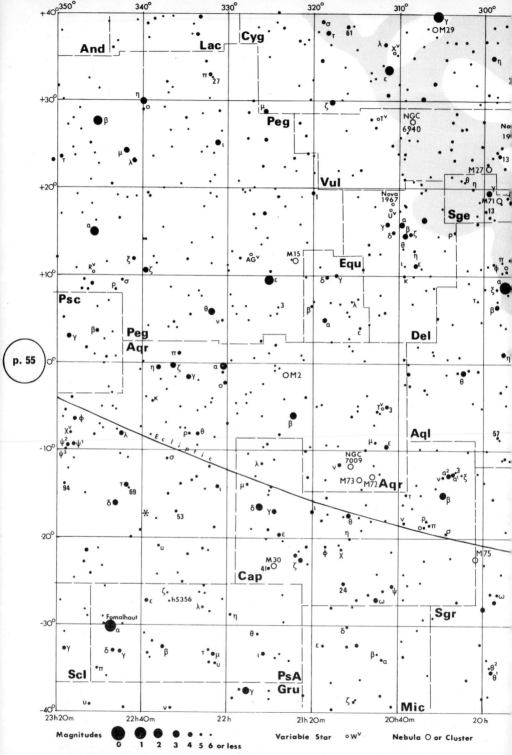

Fig. 28 Equatorial Stars (RA 16ʰ to 23ʰ 20ᵐ).

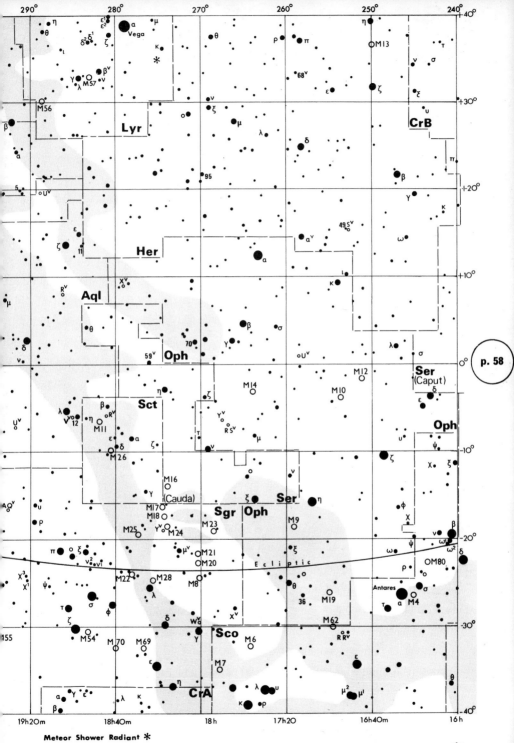

Meteor Shower Radiant ✳

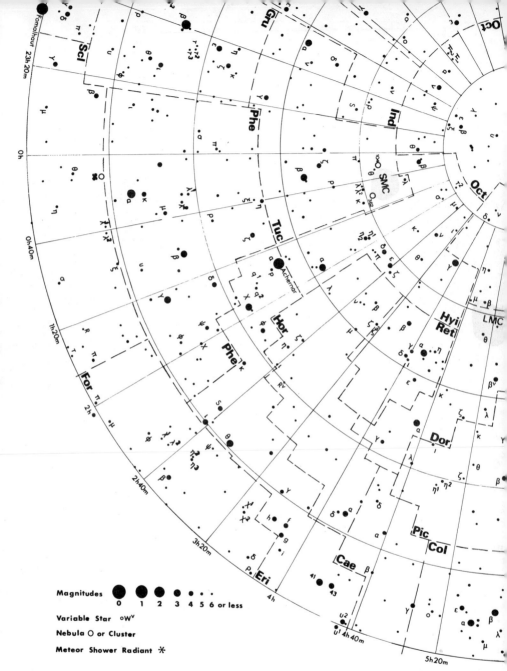

Magnitudes

| 0 | 1 | 2 | 3 | 4 5 6 or less |

Variable Star oWᵛ

Nebula O or Cluster

Meteor Shower Radiant ✳

Fig. 29   Southern Stars (RA 23ʰ 20ᵐ to 12ʰ 40ᵐ).

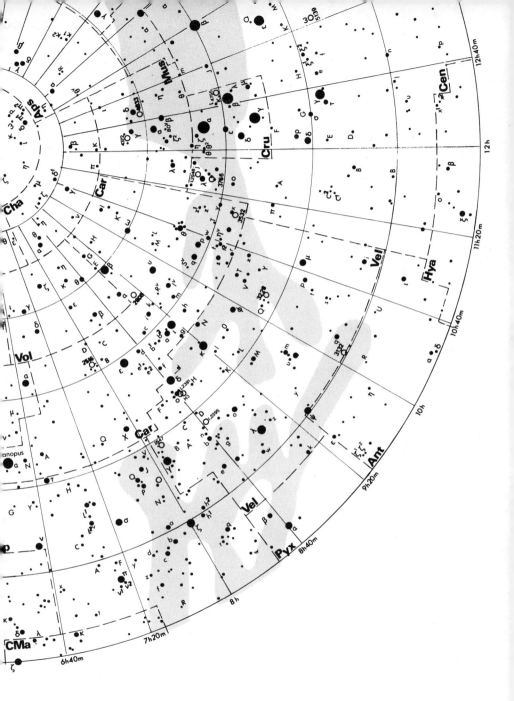

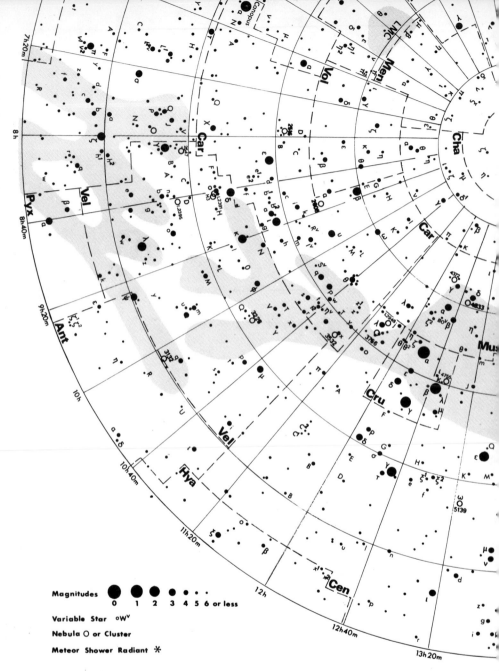

Magnitudes ● ● ● ● ● · ·
           0 1 2 3 4 5 6 or less

Variable Star ○W^v

Nebula ○ or Cluster

Meteor Shower Radiant ✳

Fig. 30 **Southern Stars (RA 7ʰ 20ᵐ to 20ʰ 40ᵐ).**

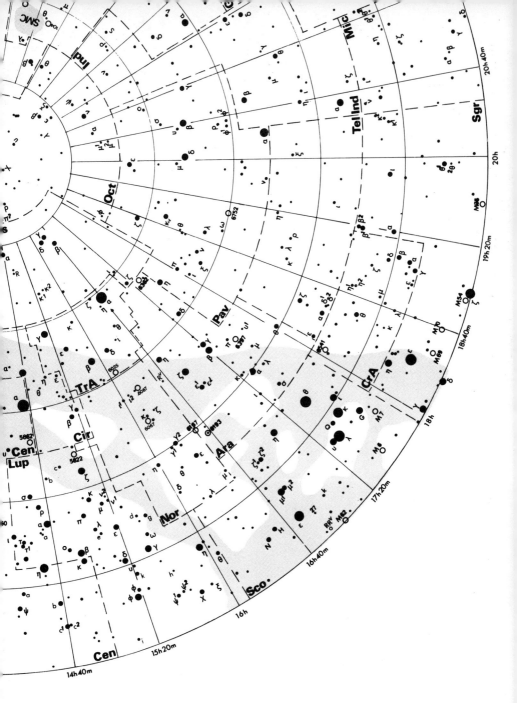

65

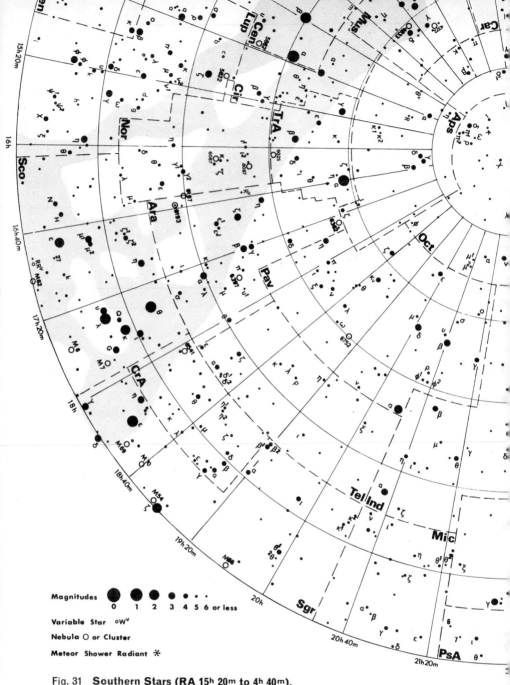

Fig. 31　Southern Stars (RA 15ʰ 20ᵐ to 4ʰ 40ᵐ).

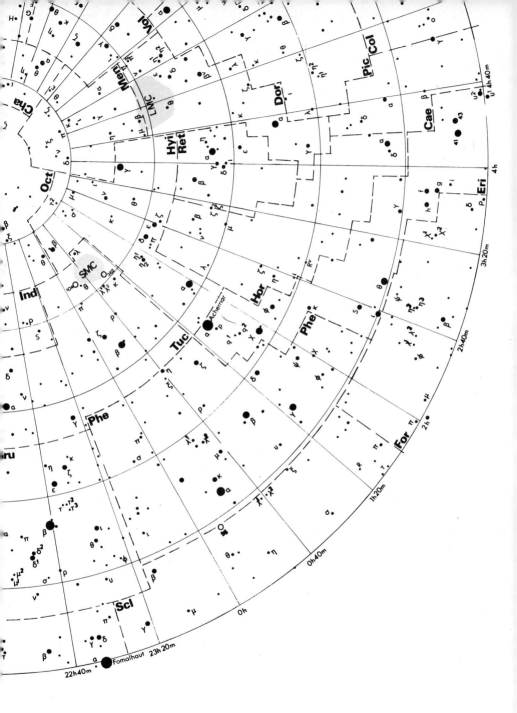

67

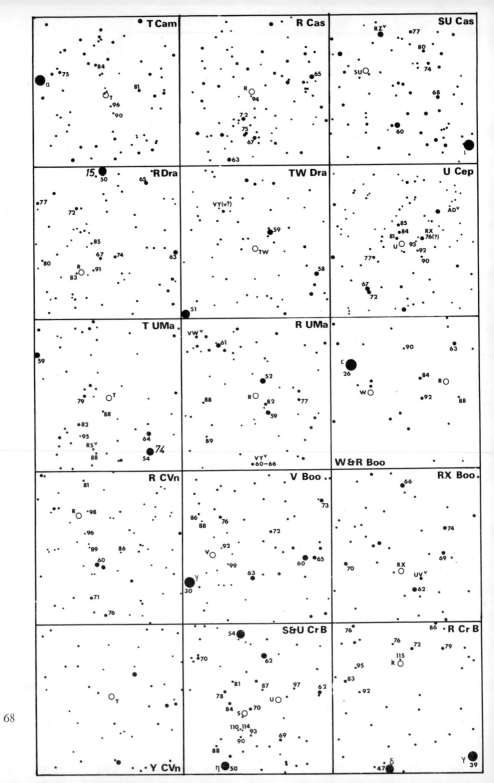

Fig. 39. Variable Stars (Finder Charts)

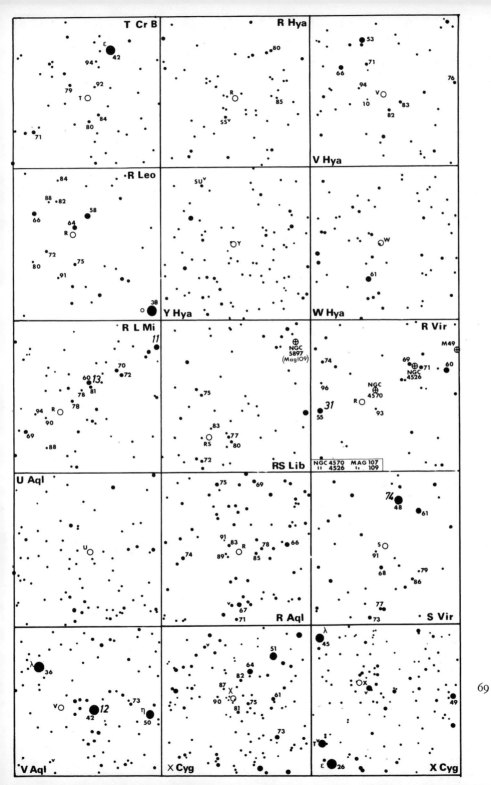

Fig. 33 Variable Stars (Finder Charts).

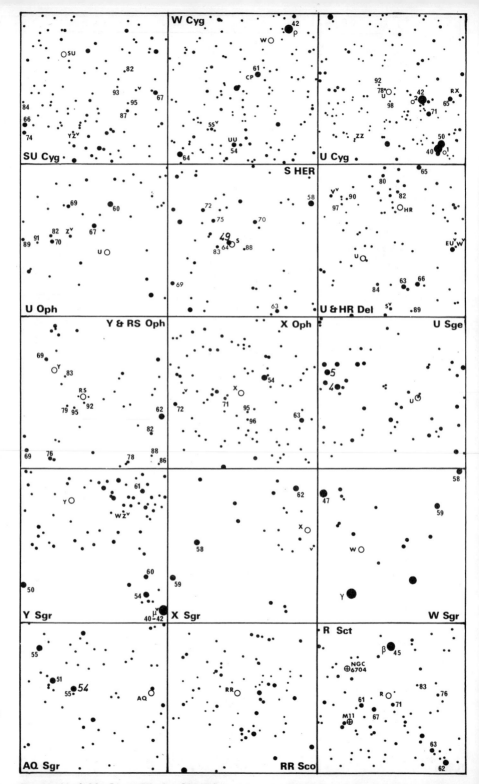

Fig. 34 Variable Stars (Finder Charts).

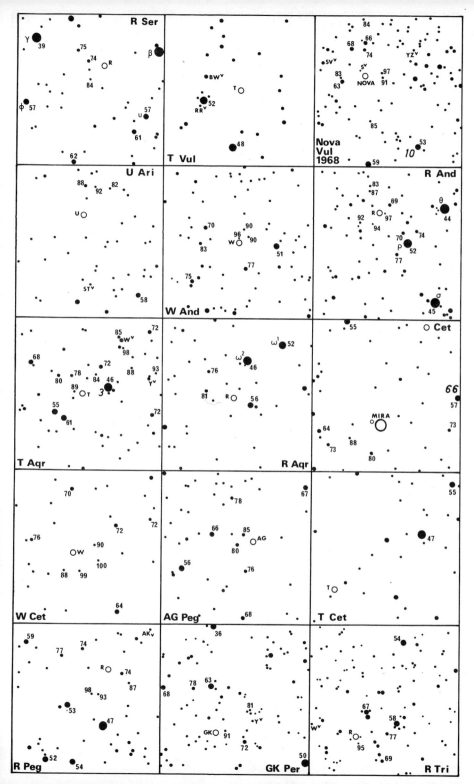

Fig. 35 Variable Stars (Finder Charts)

71

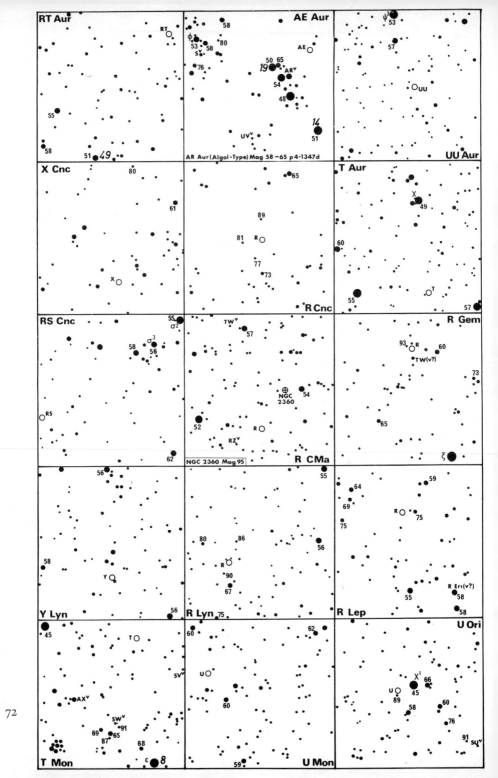

72

Fig. 36 Variable Stars (Finder Charts).

continued from p.47

Index Catalogue (IC. or I.1000); in some of the southern hemisphere deep-sky charts the prefix NGC is omitted, and only the number is given. Individual stars (apart from using their Arabic names) are identified by a Greek letter (Bayer's method), by a number only (Flamsteed's number), by a Roman letter (usually Lacaille's and Gould's southern stars) or by the numbering adopted in specialist catalogues such as Sir John Herschel's (Hh), W. S. Jacob's (Jc), or F. G. W. Struve's (Σ). When using a Greek letter for a star, the name of the constellation is in the genitive, e.g. α Ursae Majoris (or its official abbreviation α UMa). (For variable stars see p. 27.)

period
With variable stars, this refers to the period of light variations when known, and in the case of binary (double) stars the period of their orbital revolution.

U.T.
Astronomers use several different kinds of time, but for convenience they use Universal Time (U.T.) (=Greenwich Time) almost exclusively in tables and ephemerides. Universal Time is independent of the observer's longitude, or local time (unless they happen to coincide).

Variable Star Finder Charts (pp. 68–72)
When these are included for a particular interesting deep-sky variable star, each small square represents an area of sky measuring approximately $3° \times 3°$ (with north uppermost). The position of the variable is indicated by a small circle. The brighter field stars included assist identification and enable magnitude estimates to be made.

To find a deep sky variable, first locate its general position on the relevant deep-sky chart. Then, with binoculars or a small telescope, identify the brighter field stars—remembering to allow time for the eyes to adapt fully to night vision—using a dimmed red-tinted lamp when referring to the star charts. If the star is a long period variable (LPV), it may be at minimum brightness and therefore temporarily beyond range of binoculars or small telescopes.

In the finder charts the small number appearing alongside a comparison star refers to its magnitude. The decimal point is omitted between the whole magnitude number and the tenths so as to avoid ambiguity with faint stars, e.g. 93 = mag 9·3. Most of the stars in the finder charts are below naked-eye visibility.

The faintest stars shown are about mag 10, but in some charts of the brighter selected variables the fainter stars are omitted, since they are not required for purposes of identification.

Refer also to Chart Legends.

Constellation Descriptions

Northern Constellations

Andromeda (And) *The Chained Lady*

A long constellation best located either from Perseus to the east or Pegasus west of it. Actually α Andromedae is a star 'borrowed' by Pegasus in order to create the distinctive 'Square' and is located at its north-east corner.

In mythology, Andromeda was the beautiful daughter of Cepheus and Cassiopeia; she was ordered to be exposed to a sea-monster as a sacrifice. To this end she was chained to a rock to await his arrival, but Perseus came across her in the nick of time, rescued her and killed the monster. This legend was so firmly established by the first century A.D., that Josephus wrote that both the links of Andromeda's chain and the bones of the sea-monster might be seen in the star configurations!

Brightest stars: α And *Alpheratz*, mag 2·2, blue-white; a spectroscopic binary and the larger component is over 175 times more luminous than the Sun. β *Mirach*, mag 2·4, orange-red. γ *Alamac*, mag 2·9, white.

Deep-sky objects: M 31, a spiral galaxy, 'the Great Nebula in Andromeda'; (Pl. 8) plainly visible to the naked eye as a 4th-magnitude (4·8) hazy spot and undoubtedly it was noticed by the first stargazers thousands of years ago; even in 8 × 30 binoculars its length can be traced (using averted vision) out to nearly 4° (or eight times the apparent diameter of the full moon to the naked eye); it represents one of the nearest 'island universes' lying at a distance of over 2 million light years. Near by is M 32, an elliptical galaxy closely related to M 31 and in the same field of view with low power instruments; however, it is not visible in small binoculars, but a 2-in telescope will show it as a hazy star-like object; mag 8·5, dia 1·5′.

Meteor shower: the *Andromedids* (or Bielids); these reach maximum activity about 14 November each year and appear to emerge from a radiant point near and north of γ Andromedae. This shower has been traced back to A.D. 524 and gave rise to great displays in 1872 and 1885; it has some connection with Biela's famous comet which divided into two parts in 1846; although it returned to the Sun in 1852, still as two separate comets, it has not been observed since.

Auriga (Aur) *The Charioteer*

Located mid-way between Perseus and Ursa Major and easily found owing to its distinctive polygon shape and the prominent 1st-magnitude star Capella.

In mythology there are conflicting stories, but it is usually identified with Amalthea, who with her sister Melissa fed Jupiter with goat's milk during his infancy.

Brightest stars: α Aur *Capella*, 'the Little She-Goat', mag 0·2, yellow. In Europe it used to be nicknamed 'the Shepherd's Star'; it was also an important calendar star to the Megalithic astronomers. β *Menkalinan*, mag 2·1, white. γ *El Nath* (β Tau), a star common to both Auriga and Taurus; mag 1·8, blue-white.

Deep-sky objects: M 36, an open cluster, mag 6·3, dia 12'. M 37, an open cluster, mag 6·2, dia 20'. M 38, an open cluster, mag 7·4, dia 20'. All three clusters are plainly visible in binoculars. RT, a Cepheid-type variable, mag range 5·4–6·6, period 3·7 d, yellowish white.

Boötes (Boo) *The Herdsman*

An easily recognizable constellation, dominated by the 1st magnitude star Arcturus. In the northern hemisphere it is visible for much of the year. With Spica (α Vir) and Denebola (β Leo) it forms a distinct equilateral triangle.

In mythology Boötes is a rustic character holding a club or spear but occasionally a staff or sickle. He may also appear holding in leash the two hunting dogs (Canes Venatici).

Brightest stars: α Boo *Arcturus*—a name probably due to confusion with the Arcas story of the Bears; mag 0·2, yellow-orange; a giant star and the fifth brightest in the entire heavens; in 1933 the light of Arcturus was used to trigger off the lights of the Chicago World's Fair. β *Nakkar*, mag 3·6, yellow. γ *Seginus*, mag 3·0, white. δ, mag 3·5, yellow. ε *Pulcherrima*, mag 2·6, yellow-orange. η *Muphrid*, mag 2·8, yellow.

Deep-sky objects: κ Boo, easy double for 2-in telescopes, mags 6·6 and 4·6, dist 13". V, LPV, mag range 6·4–11·5, period 258·81 d. ν, triple system but only double in binoculars, mags 4·5 and 6·7, white and yellow, dist 108".

Camelopardalis (Cam) *The Giraffe*

A long, straggling modern constellation formed in 1614. It stretches from a point near the Pole Star, and its major part lies between Ursa Major and Cassiopeia. It contains no star brighter than the 4th magnitude, and the very barrenness of the sky to the naked eye in this part of the northern heavens serves as a good guide to its location.

Although it is a new constellation in the Western World, the ancient Chinese named seven asterisms in this part of the sky.

Brightest stars: α Cam, mag 4·4, blue. β, mag 4·2, yellow. γ, mag 4·7, white. Deep-sky objects: 11 and 12 Cam, a wide binocular double; mags 5·3 and 6·0, blue and yellow, dist 180″. T, LPV, mag range 6·4–14·4, period 373 d, deep red. NGC 1502, an open cluster, mag 5·3, dia 7′; c. 15 stars visible with binoculars.

Canes Venatici (CVn)   *The Hunting Dogs*

Apart from its principal star, Cor Caroli, there is little to see with the naked eye, but with large telescopes the whole region is strewn with spiral galaxies.

The northernmost of the mythical dogs is called *Asterion* and the southernmost *Chara*. The hunting dogs are supposedly barking at the Great Bear. Traditionally they are in the charge of Boötes, who holds them on leads as they chase the Bear round the pole; for this reason Boötes has been nicknamed the Bear Driver.

Brightest stars: α CVn *Cor Caroli*, named in honour of Charles II of England in 1660 because the star supposedly shone with special brilliance on the evening of the King's return to London in May of that year. Also a double visible with 2-in telescopes; mags 2·9 and 5·4, both white, dist 20″.

Deep-sky objects: 15 and 17 CVn, a wide (optical) double, mags 6·2 and 6·0, dist 290″, blue and yellow-white.

γ, semi-regular variable, mag range 5·2–6·6, period 158 d, deep red; named *La Superba* by the famous Jesuit astronomer-priest Father Secchi because of its brilliant, intense red colour. M 3, globular cluster, visible in binoculars when it appears as a faint, misty blob; mag 6·4, dia 10′.

Cassiopeia (Cas)   *The Lady on the Chair or Throne*

After the Great Bear, this is probably the most easily recognizable constellation in the northern heavens. Its brightest stars form a configuration in the shape of a badly formed 'W' or 'M'—depending on which side of the pole it is seen. It may be quickly located by remembering it always lies on the opposite side of the Pole Star to the Great Bear. It is also a northern star-clock constellation (*see* p. 140).

In legend it belongs to the 'Royal Family' of constellations, and supposedly Cassiopeia was the wife of King Cepheus and the mother of Andromeda.

Brightest stars: α Cas *Schedar* or *Shadar*, an irregular variable star, mag range 2·5–3·1, orange-yellow. β *Caph*, mag 2·4, yellow-white. γ, an irregular variable, mag range 1·6–3·0, blue-white. δ *Ruchbah*, mag 2·8, white.

Deep-sky objects: R Cas, LPV, mag range 4·8–13·6, period 430 d, deep red. SU, Cepheid-type variable, mag range 5·9–6·3, period 1·9493 d, yellow-white. M 52, open cluster, mag 7·3, dia 12'. M 103, open cluster, mag 7·4, dia 5'.

Note: 'Tycho's star', which burst into view in November 1572, is one of the most famous stars on record. For a time it was visible in daylight, but then gradually faded beyond visibility. Novae, or exploding stars, sometimes recur so that the location of Tycho's star is worth watching (*see* map).

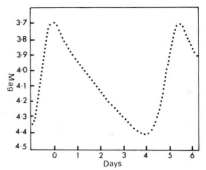

Fig. 37 Light curve of a typical Cepheid-type variable.

Cepheus (Cep)   *The Warrior King*

A relatively inconspicuous group to the casual eye and during periods near full moon it may be difficult to spot. In northern temperate latitudes of Europe and North America it is circumpolar, and as a consequence of this one sees at different times a complete inversion of the star grouping.

In legend the origin of Cepheus is controversial. Traditionally he is supposed to immortalize an ancient king who reigned either in 'Ethiopia' or India.

Brightest stars: α Cep *Alderamin,* mag 2·6, white; owing to precession (*see* p. 25) it was the Pole Star in 21000 B.C. and will be Polaris again in A.D. 7500. β *Alfirk,* a Cepheid-type variaable, mag range 3·3–3·7, period 0·1905 d, blue-white. γ *Errai,* mag 3·4, orange-yellow; it will be the Pole Star 2,600 years from now. δ, the proto-type δ Cepheid-type variable and first to be recognized by the English deaf mute John Goodricke in 1784; mag range 3·9–5·0, period 5·3663 d, yellow.

Deep-sky objects: U, an eclipsing binary variable; mag range 6·7–9·8, period 2·4929 d, blue-white to yellow. μ, a red variable, nicknamed the 'Garnet Star' by Sir William Herschel, mag range 3·6–5·1, period between 5 and 6 years; to see the red colour at its best, use binoculars to compare it with the brilliant whiteness of α Cep near by.

Cygnus (Cyg)   *The Swan or Northern Cross*

One of the easiest groups to recognize owing to its highly distinctive shape as a cross. It lies east of Vega (α Lyr), and its principal star, Deneb (α Cyg), forms, with Vega and Altair, a well-known stellar triangle. Since it is immersed in the star clouds of the Milky Way, even the simplest optical aid shows the milky background resolved into thousands of stars; in addition there is an extensive list of

77

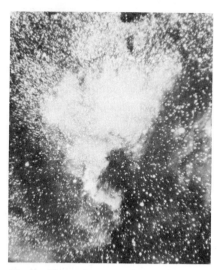

Fig. 38   The North America Nebula in Cygnus.

interesting binocular and telescopic deep-sky objects (*see* below and chart).

In mythology it was seen as a flying swan, sometimes associated with the Argonauts; to others it was just a bird; the Arabs recognized it as a 'Flying Eagle' or 'the Hen'.

Brightest stars: α Cyg *Deneb*, mag 1·3; a giant white star and among the most luminous known—giving out over 8,000 times more light than the Sun. β *Albireo*, mag 3·0; also a beautiful coloured binary system well seen in 2-in telescopes, mags 3·2 and 5·3, dist 34″, yellow (gold) and blue. γ *Sadr*, mag 2·3, yellow-white. ε *Gienah*, mag 2·6, yellow-orange.

Deep-sky objects: o², a wide triple system, mags 4·0, 5·5, 7·5, dist 358″ and 107″; an ideal 8 × 30 binocular subject. 61, a binary system, mags 5·6

and 6·3, dist 28″, yellow-orange and orange-red; a star of great historic interest, since it was the first star to have its distance measured by trigonometrical means by the German astronomer Bessel in 1838 who found it to lie 10 light years' distance away. χ, LPV, mag range 2·3–14·3, period 407 days, orange-red. X, Cepheid-type variable, mag range 5·9–7·0, period 16·3866 d, yellow; ideal for study with binoculars. M 39, an open cluster; visible in opera glasses; mag 5·2, dia 30′. NGC 7000, a gaseous nebula known as the North America Nebula owing to its distinctive geographical appearance (Fig. 38); when the sky is very dark and transparent, it can be picked out with binoculars.

Draco (Dra)   *The Dragon*

One of the more sprawling configurations in the northern skies and for most of its length wanders serpent-like between the two Bears. The head of the mythological serpent is formed by β, γ, ξ, ν and μ.

In mythology it was the monster which protected the golden apples in the garden of the Hesperides and was later slain by Hercules. In ancient China this constellation became a national emblem.

Brightest stars: α Dra *Thuban*, mag 3·6, white; this was the Pole Star about 4,700 years ago. β *Rastaban*, mag 3·0, yellow. γ *Eltamin*, mag 2·4, orange-yellow; observations of the position of this star led James Bradley, the third Astronomer Royal, to discover the aberration of light in 1725.

Meteor showers: ζ *Draconids*, reach maximum activity about 10 October each year; this shower has some connection with the Giacobini-Zinner periodic comet. ι *Draconids*, reach maximum about 30 June and they are associated with the Pons-Winnecke periodic comet. *Quadrantids*, reach maximum 2–3 January; this is the only meteor shower which carries a different name from the constellation in which the radiant is located; the reason is that it lies in a part of the sky previously occupied by the constellation Quadrans Muralis—the Mural Quadrant—invented by the French astronomer Lalande. Nowadays it is no longer recognized and has been incorporated into Draco and Boötes.

Hercules (Her)

A major constellation which covers an extended area of sky yet, surprisingly, contains no star brighter than the 3rd magnitude. It is readily found lying between Lyra and the Northern Crown. To northern observers it is very distinctive owing to the 'flowerpot' shape made by four of its principal stars.

In the earliest cultures he was depicted as a youth or kneeling giant, but in more modern times he is always identified with the 'twelve labours' of Hercules. In classical mythology, Hercules was reputed to possess great strength and courage, and one of his feats was the destruction of the dragon which guarded the garden of the Hesperides (*see* also Draco).

Brightest Stars: α Her *Ras Algethi*; a close binary system; the primary star is an orange-red giant and an irregular variable 700 times more luminous than the Sun; mags 3·1–3·9 and 5·4, dist 4·6″. β *Korneforos*, mag 2·8, yellow. γ, a double for 2-in telescopes; mags 3·8 and 8, white and blue, dist 40″.

Deep-sky objects: 68, β Lyrae-type variable, mag range 4·6–5·1, period 2·051 d, blue-white; light variations can be followed with either the naked eye or binoculars. 30, a semi-regular red giant variable; mag range 4·6–6·0, period 80 d(?); also a naked-eye or binocular star. M 13, a globular cluster; known as 'the Great Cluster of Hercules'; it consists of many thousands of stars—perhaps more than 100,000 (Pl. 2); mag 5·7, dia 10′; easily located between η and ζ and even in small opera glasses it will show up as a nebulous star; with a 6-in telescope the individual stars are resolved into myriads of scintillating, separate jewel points. M 92, a globular cluster; another bright object and easily located with binoculars; mag 6·1, dia 8′.

Lacerta (Lac) *The Lizard*

A small constellation introduced by Hevelius in the seventeenth century. It is located between Cygnus and Andromeda. It has no star brighter than the 4th magnitude.

When Hevelius formed the group, it was given an alternative name of Stellio, a newt of the Mediterranean coasts. It formed part of the ancient Chinese constellation of the Flying Serpent.

Brightest stars: α Lac, mag 3·8, white. β, mag 4·6, yellow-orange.

Deep-sky object: NGC 7243, an open cluster, mag 7·4, dia 20'; it can be picked up as a faint haze with 8 × 30s in exceptionally transparent skies.

Lynx (Lyn) *The Lynx or Tiger*

A dull, and to the naked eye, uninteresting northern group. It can be located lying half-way between Castor and Pollux (in Gemini) and the distinctive 'bowl' of Ursa Major. This is one of the modern constellations introduced by Hevelius to 'organize' stars in a part of the sky unformed by the ancients. Kepler's son-in-law, Bartschius, referred to it as 'spots on the Tiger'.

Brightest stars: α Lyn, mag 3·3, orange.

Lyra (Lyr) *The Harp or Lyre*

Although among the smallest constellations, it is one of the easiest to recognize, since with a little imagination the compact group of its brightest stars clearly depicts the Lyre or Harp. The entire group is dominated by the blazing blue-white Vega, which is located at the apex of a bold triangle with Polaris and Arcturus forming the base.

In mythology it represents the Lyre or Harp invented by Hermes and given to his half-brother Apollo, who in turn gave it to his son Orpheus, the musician of the Argonauts.

Brightest stars: α Lyr *Vega*, mag 0·1, a brilliant blue-white; it was the first star ever captured on the daguerreotype photographic plate in 1850; it was an important calendar star to the Australian Aborigines and the Romans but earlier still, in about 2000 B.C., to the sophisticated Megalithic astronomers of North West Europe; owing to precession it will become the Pole Star in approximately 11,500 years from now. β *Sheliak*, *Shelyak* or *Shiliak*, a variable star, mag range 3·4–4·3; it is the prototype β Lyra-type variety; the light variations are subject to two unequal minima (3·8 and 4·1) separated by two equal maxima (3·4) over a cycle of 12·9080 d (*see* Fig. 4); this system is of great interest, and some believe that more than two large bodies may be present; since its discovery in 1784, the period of light variations has been lengthening at a rate of two minutes per annum. δ^{1-2}, a wide, naked-eye optical double; δ^1, mag 5·5; δ^2 is also an irregular variable, mag range 4·5–6·5, blue-white and orange-red. ζ, mag 4·1; also a wide double for 2-in telescopes; mags 4·3 and 5·9, both white, dist 43″. *Deep-sky objects:* ε¹ and ε², a double-double system; the principal pair are 207″ apart, and some keen-eyed observers have claimed to have separated them with the naked eye; a 2-in telescope and a fairly high magnification will separate each star into a binary pair (mags 4·6, 6·3, dist 2·9″; mags 4·9, 5·2, dist 2·3″, yellow). R, a variable star, mag range 4·0–5·0, period 50 d, orange-red; it can be followed with the naked eye, but binoculars show the reddish colour to best advantage. M 56, a globular cluster, mag 8·2, dia 2′; although faint, it can be glimpsed with 7 × 35s when the atmosphere is very transparent—especially if averted vision is used (*see* p. 35). M 57, a planetary nebula, mag 9·3, size 83″ × 59″; the famous Ring Nebula (Fig. 39); in spite of its faintness it can just be detected as a small, hazy star in 2-in telescopes. *Meteor shower:* the *Lyrids*; these are active at maximum 19 and 20 April each year from a radiant situated 5° south-west of Vega, and are associated with the orbit of Comet 1861 I.

Perseus (Per)

This northern constellation is a member of the Royal Family of constellations and is located between the conspicuous 'W' of Cassiopeia and the striking 1st-magnitude white star Capella (α Aur).

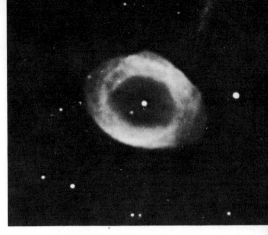

Fig. 39   The Ring Nebula (M 57) in Lyra.

In the past, Perseus was called 'the Bearer of the Demon's Head', and in this role he is associated with one of the best known and most romantic Greek legends (*see* Andromeda p. 74). *Brightest stars:* α Per *Algenib* or *Marfak*, mag 1·9, yellow-white. β *Algol*, known as 'the Demon Star'; this is the best known object in the constellation; it is an eclipsing variable star of a kind of which over a thousand are known to exist within the Milky Way. The Arabs called it Al Gol (or El Ghoul), the spirit or demon, and it seems that they knew about its variable nature. Actually it consists of a two- or possibly three-star system which is not fully understood since the eclipsing star undergoes unpredictable changes (Fig. 40 shows the possible two-star configuration); mag range 2·2–3·5, period 2·8673 d. *Deep-sky objects:* ρ Per, a semi-regular variable; mag range 3·2–3·8, orange-red (located near Algol). NGC 869

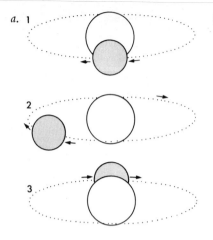

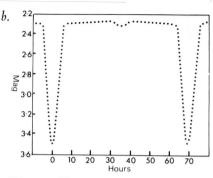

Fig. 40 a. The two-star configuration of Algol (β Per) showing why the periodic light variations occur; 1. Minimum; 2. Maximum; 3. Slight dip.

Fig. 40 b. Light curve of Algol.

and 884, the famous 'double cluster' or 'Sword Hand of Perseus'; mags 4·4 and 4·7, dia both 36'; both are visible to the naked eye as nebulous smudges, and with opera glasses or binoculars their double nature is resolved. M 34, an open cluster, mag 5·5, dia 18'. *Note:* Several other clusters in this group are visible in binoculars (*see* chart).

Meteor shower: the *Perseids*; a shower which provides displays between 25 July and 17 August each year from a radiant between χ and η Persei; this shower was known in the Middle Ages as 'the Tears of St Lawrence'. The meteoroid paths follow the orbit of Comet 1862 III, which has a period of 122 years.

Ursa Major (UMa)   *The Great Bear*

This is the best known constellation in the northern skies. In addition to the name of the Bear, it is also known alternatively as the Plough, the Dipper,

Charles's Wain, the Chariot or Wagon or the Bier.

In Greek mythology the Great Bear is closely associated with the Little Bear and is connected with the story of the nymph Callisto, to whom Jupiter was over-attentive. Juno, Jupiter's wife, became jealous and transformed both Callisto and her son Arcas into bears. Later Jupiter made them into constellations where he could watch over them.

Brightest stars: α UMa *Dubhe*, mag 2·0, yellowish-orange; with β it forms 'the Pointers'; a line projected from β to α and then extended about five times the length between the two stars finds the position of the Pole Star. β *Merak*, mag 2·4, white. γ *Phad* or *Phekda*, mag 2·5, white. δ *Megrez*, mag 3·4, white; the faintest member of the seven-star group forming the Plough. ε *Alioth*, mag 1·7, white. ζ *Mizar*, mag 2·2, white; it forms a naked-eye double with the companion star *Alcor*, mag 4·0, white, dist 11'; it was once supposed by the Arabs to be a test for naked-eye acuity; in binoculars another fainter star can be seen (Fig. 41) which is known by the name Sidus Ludovicianum; it was named by an eccentric German amateur in 1723 who thought he had discovered a new planet and named it to honour Ludwig V; *Mizar* is also a double system which can be seen in 2-in telescopes, mags 2·4 and 4·0, dist 14·5″.

Deep-sky objects: M 81 and M 82, two galaxies which lie within $\frac{1}{2}$° of each other and can be glimpsed with 8 × 30 binoculars on clear, moonless nights; in 1961 it was found that the two galaxies are physically connected.

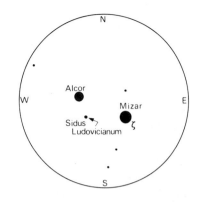

Fig. 41   *The starfield ζ UMa.*

Ursa Minor (UMi)   *The Lesser Bear*

This represents one of the most important groups in the entire heavens since it contains the present Pole Star (Polaris), which is situated so close to the true north pole as to make the location of true north a simple matter. The Arabs nicknamed Polaris 'the Guiding One'. The two brightest stars β and γ are referred to as 'the Guards' or 'the Guardians of the Pole'.

In mythology the group commemorates Arcas, the son of Callisto (*see* Ursa Major). In North America, the Red Indians knew it as a young girl who guided a party of hunting braves.

Brightest stars: α UMi *Alruccabah* or Polaris, Stella Polaris, the Pole Star, mag 2·1, yellow; the Chinese named it after Tou Mu who had supernatural powers and saved sailors from shipwreck. β *Kochab*, mag 2·2, orange-yellow. γ with 11 UMi form a wide binocular double, mags 3·1 and 5·1, white and orange-yellow, with β it forms 'the Guardians'; in primitive civilizations the two stars were used as a clock (*see* also p. 139).

Deep-sky objects: π^1, a double visible in 2-in telescopes, mags 6·1 and 7·0, dist 31″.

Equatorial Constellations

Antlia (Ant) *The Air Pump*

An inconspicuous constellation between Hydra and Vela introduced by Lacaille under the name Machina Pneumatica about 1752 to commemorate the Air Pump of Robert Boyle.

Brightest stars: α Ant, mag 4·4, orange-red. ε, mag 4·6, orange-red.

Deep-sky objects: S, β Lyra-type variable, mag range 6·4–6·8, period 0·6483 d, white; this binary system has one of the shortest periods known (7 hrs 47 mins); although the variation in brightness is only about half a magnitude, it can be detected using opera glasses or binoculars. NGC 3132, a small planetary nebula just visible in 2-in telescopes, using a moderate power; mag 8·2, size 80″ × 50″; the associated star (mag 10·6) requires at least 3-in aperture.

Aquarius (Aqr) *The Water Bearer*

The eleventh of the zodiacal groups. Although it has no star brighter than magnitude 3, it has its fair share of interesting binocular and telescopic subjects. The group is best located by projecting a line due south of the Pegasus 'Square' or north of the 1st-magnitude star Fomalhaut (α Piscis Austrini).

In mythology, the Water Bearer is represented with a bucket or urn which he holds on his shoulder. Most early civilizations seem to have an Aquarius legend in some way associated with water or liquid in various forms ranging from rain and great floods to wine. The old astrologers said that Sadalmelik (α Aqr) was an extremely lucky star, and several others stars of the group were also considered lucky.

Brightest stars: α Aqr *Sadalmelik*, mag 3·2, yellow. β *Sadalsund*, mag 3·1, yellow. γ *Sadachbia*, mag 4·0, white. δ, mag 3·5, white.

Deep-sky objects: ψ² Aqr, a double system, mags 4·5 and 8·5, dist 50″, yellow and blue; a beautiful object for 2-in telescopes. M 2, a globular cluster, mag 6·3, dia 8′; a bright, easy object for binoculars appearing as a nebulous star; in a small telescope it has been described as 'a heap of glittering fine sand'. NGC 4628, a planetary nebula, 'the Saturn Nebula', so called owing to its vague similarity to a hazy telescopic depiction of the famous ringed planet; mag 8·4, size 44″ × 26″; it requires at least a 2–2½-in telescope with a power of × 50 or greater.

Meteor shower: δ Aquarids; a display observable each year between 15 July and 10 August (at its peak on 29 July) radiating slow-moving meteors from a position near the star δ Aqr. This shower is also connected with the Arietid meteor stream.

Aquila (Aql) *The Eagle*

A conspicuous constellation dominated by the brilliant blue-white stars Altair (α Aql), β and γ which give the figure a distinctive, easily recognized pattern.

In mythology Aquila was a bird. The Greeks said it represented the eagle which brought nectar to Jupiter while he lay concealed in a cave in Crete. Another story associates it with Prometheus, and yet another with Zeus. The group is represented on a Babylonian 'boundary' stone dated about 1200 B.C. and later on several Roman coins.

Brightest stars: α Aql *Altair*; named as the Flying Vulture or Eagle, the same title as the constellation; mag 0·9, white. β *Alshain*, mag 3·3, yellow. γ *Tarazed*, mag 2·8, orange-yellow; with α and β it forms a convenient celestial measuring rod almost exactly 5° in length. δ, mag 3·0, blue-white. η, a Cepheid-type variable, mag range 3·9–5·1, period 7·1766 d, yellow; a star which can be studied with either the naked eye or binoculars.

Deep-sky objects: U, a Cepheid-type variable, mag range 6·2–6·9, period 7·0238 d, yellow; an ideal binocular subject. V, an irregular variable, mag range 6·7–8·2, deep orange-red; another 8 × 30 binocular star. *Note:* As the constellation lies in the Milky Way, novae, or exploding stars, are not uncommon; since 1899 at least four have been discovered; chances of making new discoveries are always good for naked-eye or binocular observers who maintain a careful watch on this part of the heavens.

Aries (Ari) *The Ram*

The first sign of the Zodiac; the point where, in a very significant period of ancient history, the Sun was located at the time of the spring equinox. Nowadays, owing to precession, this point has shifted into Pisces, although by tradition the vernal equinox is still referred to as the first point in Aries. Since Aries is not a prominent group, it is best located by bisecting a line connecting the 'Square' of Pegasus and Aldebaran (α Tau).

In mythology the constellation is closely associated with the Argonauts and symbolizes the ram which bore the golden fleece which the expedition set out to seek. It was a dreaded sign of the old astrologers, and Pliny wrote that if a comet appeared there, it portended great wars and widespread mortality.

Brightest stars: α Ari *Hamal*, mag 2·2, yellow-orange. β *Sheratan*, mag 2·7, white. γ *Mesarthim*, mag 4·0, white; it was the first double system discovered, by the Englishman Robert Hooke in 1664 and he goes on record as remarking: 'I took notice that it consisted of two small stars very near together; a like instance to which I have not else met with in all the heavens'; mags 4·8 and 4·8, both white, dist 8″.

Caelum (Cae)   *The Engraving Tool*

One of Lacaille's new southern constellations formed in 1752. Located between Eridanus and Columba; its northern part is just visible to observers in latitudes 50° N.

It supposedly represents the engraving tool used by metal and ivory craftsmen.

Brightest stars: α Cae, mag 4·5, yellowish-white. β, mag 5·1, yellowish-white. γ, mag 4·6, yellow-orange. δ, mag 5·2, blue-white.

Cancer (Cnc)   *The Crab*

The fourth sign of the Zodiac. It contains no star brighter than 4th magnitude, but it is easily located owing to its close proximity to Leo. A line extended from Capella (α Aur) through Pollux (β Gem) indicates the direction.

In legend, Cancer was the animal sent by Juno to annoy Hercules during his combat with the Lernaean Hydra; in another legend he is represented as two asses which helped Jupiter in his victory over the giants.

Brightest stars: α Cnc *Acubens*, mag 4·3, yellowish-white. β *Al Tarf*, mag 3·8, yellow. γ *Asellus Borealis*, 'the Northern Ass Colt', mag 4·7, white. δ *Asellus Australis*, mag 4·2, yellow.

Deep-sky objects: RS, a semi-regular variable, mag range 5·5–7·0, period 253 d(?). M 44, the famous Praesepe, or Beehive Star Cluster, which is readily visible to the naked eye as a nebulous spot; this was one of the first objects which Galileo observed with his newly developed telescope; he was surprised and delighted to see it resolved into 36 separate stars; mag 3·7, dia 95″; with 10 × 50s, about 75 stars can be counted. M 67, an open cluster, mag 6·1, dia 15′; a nebulous spot in binoculars.

Canis Major (CMa)   *The Greater Dog*

A group easily located since it contains Sirius, the brightest visible star in both hemispheres, and in addition it lies just a few degrees south-east of the distinctive configuration of Orion. A line extended from the Pleiades through Orion's belt points directly towards it.

A Greek story relates that the group was named in honour of the hunting dog given by Aurora to Cephalus which was the swiftest member of the species then known.

Brightest stars: α CMa *Sirius*, the brightest star in the heavens; mag −1·37, brilliant white; the name is derived from the Greek *seirios*, 'sparkling' or 'burning'. In the Egyptian calendar when Sirius appeared in the morning sky before sunrise, it announced that the annual flooding of the Nile was about to begin. Sirius has a small companion star, Sirius 'B', which can only be seen in larger telescopes. Although it is a star only 1/10,000 as bright as the Sun, its density is 36,000 times greater. One cubic inch of Sirius 'B' weighs as much as a ton on Earth. β *Murzim*, mag 2·0, blue-white. γ *Muliphen* (or *Mirza*), mag 4·1, blue-white. δ *Wezan* mag 2·0, yellow. ε *Adara* or *Undara*, mag 1·6, blue-white.

Deep-sky objects: M 41, an open cluster, mag 4·6; a cloud of minute stars about ½° in diameter just visible to the naked eye 4° south of Sirius.

Canis Minor (CMi)   *The Little Dog*

Located south of Gemini, west of Hydra and north-east of Canis Major. Like the Greater Dog it is dominated by a bright star, Procyon, which with Betelgeuse and Sirius forms an almost equilateral triangle. Another method to locate it is by extending a line from the three stars of Orion's belt towards Sirius and dropping or raising (depending whether one is in the southern or northern hemisphere) a perpendicular which will then pass through Procyon.

To the Greek poets he was intended as one of the hounds which belonged to the pack of Orion; others say it was the faithful *Moera* which belonged to Icarius and after the death of his master threw himself down a well in his despair.

Brightest stars: α CMi *Procyon*, mag 0·5, yellow-white. β *Gomeisa*, mag 3·1, blue-white.

Deep-sky object: 14, a binocular triple, mags 6, 8, 9, dist 85″ and 117″; the stars are not physically connected.

Capricornus (Cap)   *The Goat*

The tenth zodiacal sign. Although a small constellation, it is quite a distinct group. Best found by projecting a line from Vega (α Lyr) through Altair (α Aql) and then extending it approximately the same distance southwards.

In mythology Capricornus supposedly represents the goat Amalthea which nourished Jupiter during his infancy, but this name is likely better associated with the constellation of Auriga. Another story relates it to Pan. On oriental zodiacs he is a fish swallowing an antelope. To the old astrologers, Capricornus was always considered a fortunate sign.

Brightest stars: α¹ and α² Cap *Giedi*; consists of two stars visible to the naked eye; mags α¹ 4·5, α² 3·8, both yellow, dist 6′ 16″. β *Dabih Major* and *Dabih Minor*, a wide optical double; mags 3·2 and 6·2, dist 205″. δ *Deneb Algedi*; mag 3·0, white; close by this star, J. G. Galle of the Berlin Observatory discovered the planet Neptune in 1846.

Deep-sky objects: σ, a wide optical pair, mags 5·5 and 9, dist 54″, orange-yellow and blue-white. M 30, a globular cluster, mag 5·5, dia 6′; visible as a nebulous spot with 8 × 30s near the star 41 Capricorni.

Centaurus (Cen)   *The Centaur*

A large southern constellation located between Hydra, Crux and Circinus.

It represents one of the most ancient of all constellations and is included in the *Almagest* of Ptolemy and is depicted on the Farnese globe (Fig. 42).

In mythology it is supposed to be in memory of the Centaurs, half men and half horses inhabiting Thessaly. Others, however, say that the group is in memory of Chiron, usually associated with Sagittarius (*see* p. 99).

Brightest stars: α Cen *Toliman* or *Rigel Kent*, mag 0·1, yellow; it represents one of the finest binary systems in the sky but requires at least a 3-in telescope (mags 0·3 and 1·7, dist 1·8″–2″, period 80 years). Close by to α Cen is Proxima Centauri, a faint 9th mag star but the nearest one to the Sun at a distance of 4·3 light-years. β (*Agena?*), mag 0·9, blue-white. γ, mag 2·4, white.

Deep-sky objects: ω Cen (NGC 5139), a globular cluster appearing as a star to the naked eye; mag 3·7, dia 23′; perhaps the richest globular cluster in the heavens. I.2948 (Dunlop 289), a beautiful open (binocular) cluster, dia 15′.

Cetus (Cet)   *The Whale* (or *Sea-Monster*)

An extensive constellation 50° in length and 20° in breadth, but it has no star brighter than 2nd magnitude. It lies south of Aries and Pisces and west of Eridanus in a barren area of the sky for naked-eye observers.

As a mythological whale it is often depicted as a very peculiar animal. It has the head of a dinosaur and the flippers of a walrus; in some maps he is depicted like the great bull elephant seal of the Southern and Pacific oceans. In celestial maps made by the biblical reformers, he assumed the role of the whale which swallowed Jonah. *Brightest stars:* α Cet *Menkar*, mag 2·8, orange-red. β *Diphda*, mag 2·2, yellow-orange; in ancient China it was Too Sze Kung, or 'the Super-intendent of Earthworks'. γ *Al Kaff al Jidhmah*, mag 3·6, white. ζ *Baten Kaitos*, mag 3·9, yellow-orange; with χ Ceti, mag 4·8, yellow-orange; it forms a wide naked-eye double. η *Deneb* or *Dheneb*, mag 3·6, yellow-orange.

Deep-sky objects: o *Mira* known as 'the Wonder'; a long period variable star first noticed by Fabricius in 1596. Although its magnitude normally ranges 1·7–9·6 in a period of 331 days, its maximum brightness is often no greater than magnitude 3 or 4. It possesses a wonderful reddish tint and is an ideal subject for naked-eye study, being visible for up to six months. Towards maximum it gains brightness quite rapidly and then slowly dies away again. At maximum it is 1,400 times more luminous than the Sun.

Columba (Col)   *The Dove* (*Noah's Dove*)

A constellation lying south of Orion and Lepus and introduced by Bayer

1 *Planisphere (1702) showing traditional constellation figures (top) and (below) part of the Zodiac of Backer (1680) with traditional figures reversed.*

2   ABOVE   *Globular star cluster (M 13) in Hercules.*

3   BELOW   *The Crab Nebula (M 1) in Taurus.*

4   ABOVE   *The Trifid Nebula (NGC 6514) in Sagittarius.*

5   BELOW   *The Dumb-bell Nebula (M 27) in Vulpecula.*

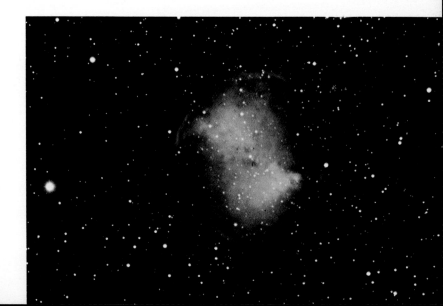

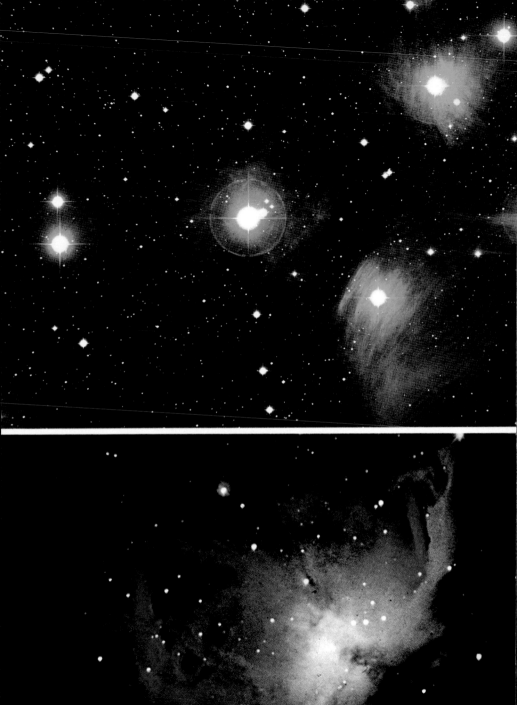

6   TOP LEFT   *The Pleiades star cluster (M 45).*

7   LEFT   *The Orion Nebula (M 42).*

8   ABOVE   *The Andromeda spiral galaxy (M 31).*
(below centre, spiral galaxy M 32;
upper right, spiral galaxy NGC 205)

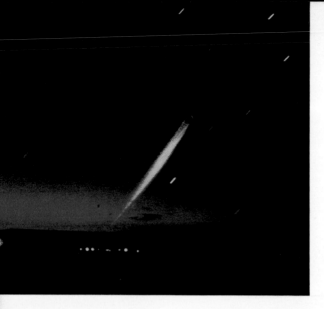

9   ABOVE   *Sungrazing Comet Ikeya-Seki 1965 f in the dawn sky.*

10   BELOW   *The Aurora Borealis (Northern Lights).*

11   ABOVE *Comet Humason 1961e. This comet had a very unusual contorted tail visible from the distance of Jupiter's orbit.*

12   BELOW *Jupiter showing cloud belts and the 'Red' Spot at the top left.*

13   *The solar system. (Planets not to scale)*

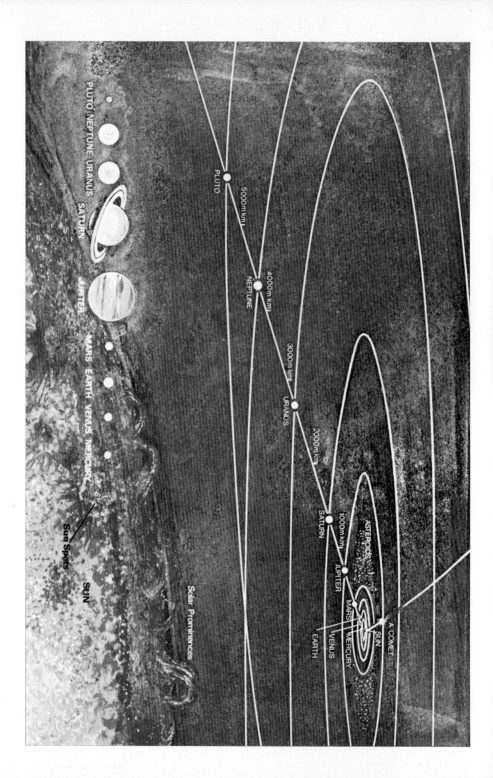

and Royer. Although primarily a southern group, part of it is observable from northern temperate latitudes. According to Sir Norman Lockyer, seven Egyptian temples were orientated towards it, but in the light of more recent thinking, this idea now seems doubtful.

Brightest stars: α Col *Phakt*, mag 2·7, blue-white. β, mag 4·4, yellow-orange. At an earlier period α and β were called 'the Good Messengers' or 'Bringers of Good News', alluding to the role played by Noah's Dove.

Coma Berenices (Com) *Berenice's Hair*

A small constellation, faint to the naked eye, appearing as a woolly aggregation of stars. Best located by projecting a line from η Ursae Majoris through α Canum Venaticorum (Cor Caroli), then halfway towards Denebola (β Leonis) lies the main body of the constellation.

Berenice's Hair relates to an old Middle Eastern legend. Berenice married her own brother Euergetes, a king of Egypt. She vowed that if her husband returned safely from a war, she would dedicate her beautiful hair to Venus. When Euergetes returned safely, Berenice, true to her promise, hung her tresses in the temple of Venus, but Jupiter was so enraptured that he immortalized them in the heavens for all to see thereafter.

Brightest stars: α Com, mag 4·5,

Fig. 42 The Atlante Farnese globe, a Roman sculpture of c. 200 BC. See p. 149.

yellow-white. β, mag 4·8, yellow. γ, mag 4·6, orange-yellow.

Deep-sky objects: 17 Com, wide binocular double, mags 5·4 and 6·7, dist 145″. M 53, globular cluster just visible on really clear, moonless nights with 10 × 50 binoculars as a hazy star; mag 7·6, dia 3·5.

Six-in telescopes will show up to about thirty spiral galaxies in the region which overlaps into Virgo.

Corona Borealis (CrB) *The Northern Crown*

One of the smallest, yet most distinctive, configurations in the northern heavens. It is easily located as a neat semi-circle of six brightish stars—appearing as a crown, or garland—one third the distance from Arcturus (α Boo) towards Vega (α Lyr).

In Greek mythology the name Corona Borealis is associated with the crown of Ariadne (daughter of Minos, King of Crete). To the Arabs it was a broken plate; to the Australian Aborigines a boomerang; while to the Shawnee Indians it was 'the Celestial Sister'.

Brightest stars: α CrB *Alphecca* nicknamed 'the Pearl', mag 2·3, white. β *Nusakan*, mag 3·7, white. γ, mag 3·9, white. δ, mag 4·7, yellow. ε, mag 4·2, yellow-orange. θ, mag 4·2, blue-white.

Deep-sky objects: U, eclipsing variable; visible through its entire range with 10 × 50s, mag range 7·6–8·9, period 3·4522 d. R, irregular variable; often remains at constant brightness for years on end; mag range 5·8–14·0. T, 'the Blaze Star'; in 1866 it suddenly brightened from a dim, mag 9·5 star to mag 2·0; as a recurring nova (exploding star) it brightened again on 8 February 1946 when it was seen almost simultaneously by a number of amateur star spotters as a mag 3 star; the location is certainly worth watching in case this star suddenly erupts again.

Corvus (Crv) *The Crow*

One of the very ancient constellations. Although rather small with few bright stars, it is easily recognized and

appears as a four-sided rhombus-like figure. It is best located by projecting a long line from Vega (α Lyr) through Spica (α Vir) and then extending it a further 15° southwards.

In mythology it may represent a Crow or a Raven. The best known story concerning the Crow is related in Ovid's *Fasti*. The principal Raven story concerns the victory of Valerius over one of the Senones.

Brightest stars: α Crv *Al Chiba*, 'the Raven or Crow', mag 4·2, yellow-white. β, mag 2·8, yellow. γ *Gienah*, mag 2·8, blue-white. δ *Algores* or *Algorab*, mag 3·1, white.

Crater (Crt) *The Cup*

Situated near Corvus in the back of Hydra, it lies due south of Leo and west of the distinctive rhombic configuration of Corvus.

One legend about it associates it with the cup which belonged to Bacchus; another with 'the Goblet of Apollo'; to the Platonists it was 'the Cup of Oblivion'.

Brightest stars: α Crt *Alkes*, mag 4·2, yellow-orange. β, mag 4·5, white. γ, mag 4·1, white. δ, mag 3·8, yellow-orange.

Delphinus (Del) *The Dolphin*

A small but highly distinctive constellation to the east of Aquila. Its four brightest stars are arranged in the shape of a diamond (Fig. 43); it has been aptly described: 'as neat as a miniature and compact as a jewel'.

Fig. 43   *Nova (HR) Delphini (arrowed), discovered by an amateur in 1967.*

In mythology Delphinus was a sacred fish and was the dolphin which saved the life of Arion, the famous lyrical poet and musician of Lesbos.

Brightest stars: α Del, mag 3·9, blue-white; although various names have been given to both α and β, none is recognized at the present time. β, mag 3·7, yellow-white. γ, mag 4·4; also a double suitable for 2-in telescopes; mags 4·5 and 5·5, dist 10″, yellow-orange and yellow-white. δ, mag 4·5, white. ε, 4·0, blue-white.

Deep-sky objects: U Del, an irregular variable, mag range 5·6–7·5, orange-red; a binocular star. HR (Nova Delphini 1967), a new 'exploding' star discovered by the British school-master, amateur star spotter G. E. D. Alcock using 11 × 80 binoculars on 8 July 1967. This star is a very unusual nova; its position should be watched carefully in the chance it may suddenly brighten again.

Equuleus (Equ)   *The Foal*

A small constellation distinguished by a trapezium of four stars of the 4th magnitude, located between Pegasus and Delphinus.

In mythology the origin of 'the Foal' is wrapped in mystery; it is not mentioned in Aratus's classic poem the *Phenomena*. However, a later and popular Greek legend relates that it is the horse Celeris given by Mercury to Castor. For northern observers, the horse is depicted inverted as is Pegasus. *Brightest stars:* α Equ *Kitalpha*, 'the Little Horse', mag 4·1, yellow-white. β, mag 5·1, white. γ, mag 4·8, yellowish-white. δ, mag 4·6, yellow-ish-white.

Eridanus (Eri) *The River*

A long winding constellation extending some 60° in length beginning from a point near the celestial equator, south of Taurus and then winding southwards to declination minus 58°. Except for Achernar (α Eri), seen only by observers in low northern latitudes, it has no star brighter than the 3rd magnitude, although the whole group has some 300 stars visible to the naked eye. It is best located by starting close by Rigel (β Ori) and then tracing the stars depicting the winding river as its twists southwards.

The classical Greek story-theme of the group concerns the daring youth Phaethon who drove the chariot of the Sun and when struck down by Jupiter by a thunderbolt (or meteorite), fell into the River Eridanus.

Brightest stars: α Eri *Achernar*, 'the End of the River', mag 0·6, blue-white; a giant star at least 200 times more luminous than the Sun. β *Cursa*, mag 2·9, white. γ *Zaurac*, 'the Bright Star of the Boat', mag 3·2, orange-red. τ¹ to τ⁹; the designation 'τ' is remarkable in that it defines nine separate stars, all between the 4th and 5th magnitudes.

Fornax (For) *The (Chemist's) Furnace*

Another of Lacaille's modern groups, dated 1752; named in honour of the great French chemist Lavoiseur. The group is situated between Eridanus and Cetus, in a comparatively barren part of the southern heavens for naked-eye stars. However, it is extremely rich in telescopic objects such as extra-galactic nebulae, and long-exposure photographs show great numbers which swarm together as 'super-clusters of island universes', vastly outnumbering the foreground stars belonging to our own Milky Way.

Brightest stars: α For, mag 4·0, yellowish-white. β, mag 4·5, yellow.

Gemini (Gem) *The Twins*

The constellation is third in order of the twelve zodiacal groups and contains some of the oldest star configurations known to mankind. It can be located by projecting a diagonal line through δ and β Ursae Majoris towards Sirius (α Canis Majoris): the twins are approximately half-way between.

The legend of the twins is considered to have its origin in the classical story of the twin sons of Jupiter and Leda which the stars Pollux and Castor represent. Castor and Pollux were regarded by both Greeks and Romans as the patrons of navigators, and this is referred to in *Acts* 28: II.

Brightest stars: α Gem *Castor*, mag 1·6, white; part of a remarkable sextuple star system. β *Pollux*, mag 1·2, yellow-orange; its colour contrasts with the whiteness of Castor. Together Pollux and Castor form a useful celestial measuring rod, for the two stars are approximately 4½° apart.

γ *Almeisan*, mag 2·2, brilliant white; near by, Max Wolf of Heidelberg detected the famous Halley's Comet on its return approach to the Sun in 1909. δ *Wasat* or *Wesat*, mag 3·5, white; close by, the new planet Pluto was first detected by the American astronomer Clyde Tombaugh in 1930. ζ *Mekbuda*, a double and a Cepheid-type variable, mag range 3·7–4·5, period 10·1535 d, yellow; the companion is mag 7, at a dist of $1\frac{1}{2}'$, an ideal binocular subject. η *Propus*, another double/variable (semiregular) combination, mags 3·2–4·2, period 230 d, orange-red, companion mag 9; near by, on 13 March 1781, William Herschel discovered the planet Uranus.

Deep-sky objects: M 35, an open cluster, mag 5·3, dia 40'; located north of η Gem; it can just be glimpsed with the unassisted eye by using averted vision; in opera glasses or binoculars it has been likened to 'a piece of frosted silver over which a twinkling light is playing'.

Meteor shower: the *Geminids*; a shower which occurs annually about 13 December from a radiant near Castor; the orbits of the meteoroid particles are smaller than any other known meteor-stream orbits; so far no comet has been associated with this shower.

Hydra (Hya)   *The Water Snake*

An extremely long constellation extending more than 100°. The head of the mythical snake begins below Cancer, and then its body winds eastwards between Leo and Virgo and ends near Libra. Its only prominent star is Alphard.

The Hydra legend is obscure. One account says that it represents the multiheaded water serpent killed by Hercules; another connects it with the legend of Corvus. Other stories identify it with any number of dragons or serpents in local folktales.

Brightest stars: α Hya *Alphard*; the great Danish astronomer Tycho Brahe (1546–1601) nicknamed it Cor Hydrae, 'the Hydra's Heart'; an alternative name is 'the Hydra's Neck; mag 2·2, yellow-orange. β, mag 4·4, blue-white. γ, mag 3·3, yellow.

Deep-sky objects: R, LPV; plainly visible to the naked eye at max; mag range 3·5–10·9, period 387 d. U, an irregular variable; ideal for naked-eye or binocular study; mag range 4·8–5·8, red. W, LPV; a binocular star; range 6·7–8·0, period 385 d. NGC 2548 (M 48(?)), a large open cluster; possibly the 'lost' Messier object number 48 which was catalogued near by; plainly visible with binoculars and appearing about the size of the full Moon to the naked eye; mag 5·3.

Leo (Leo)   *The Lion*

A very easily recognizable group because of the highly distinctive configuration of the sickle or question mark (to northern observers). The fifth sign of the Zodiac.

Fig. 44   The Leonid meteor storm of 1833.

In Greek mythology it represents the animal that inhabited the Nemaean forests. One legend associates it with the labours of Hercules. To the Hebrews it represented the Lion of Judah.

Brightest stars: α Leo *Regulus*, mag 1·3, blue-white; it was named by Copernicus 'Ruler of the Affairs of the Heavens'; to the ancients, Regulus was the leader of the four Royal Stars (Regulus, Aldebaren, Antares, Fomalhaut) which, because of their approximate equi-distance, marked off the four quarters of the celestial sphere. Since Regulus lies on the ecliptic, it is often occulted by the Moon and more rarely, but very spectacularly, by one of the planets. β *Denebola*, mag 1·6, white; whereas in ancient times astrologers considered Regulus to be of good influence, Denebola was supposedly a very unlucky star. γ *Algieba*, mag 2·3, orange-yellow. δ *Zosma* or *Duhr*, mag 2·6, white.

Deep-sky objects: τ, a wide binocular double; mags 5·5 and 7·0, dist 90", yellowish-white and blue-white. R, LPV; plainly visible with the naked eye at maximum; mag range 4·4–11·6, period 313 d, brilliant red. *Note:* with small telescopes (2½–3-in) and large binoculars (10 × 80s and 25 × 105s) at least four spiral galaxies are visible (*see* chart).

Meteor showers: the *Leonids*; these often produce the most brilliant and prolific displays seen by man in modern times. In 1966, at the height of the last big display, between 2,000 and 2,500 meteors (meteoroids) were seen every minute, and the sky was ablaze with brilliant streaks of light originating from a radiant within the sickle, a little west of ζ Leonis. The display reaches peak activity each year between 14 and 17 November. On average a normal display gives rise to about 70 meteoroids per hour. Research has shown that the Leonids were recorded as far back as A.D. 903, possibly earlier. They tend to occur in great showers (called 'storms') at intervals of thirty-three years, such as in 1799, 1833 (Fig. 44), 1866; but in

1899 and 1933 displays were poor; the 1966 display was possibly the greatest ever seen. The shower has some connection with comet 1866 I, first observed by the Chinese in 1366.

Leo Minor (LMi)   *The Lesser Lion*

One of the 'modern' constellations formed about 1690 by Hevelius; it lies between Leo and Ursa Major.

In Greek times this was an unnamed region of the heavens. The Chinese, however, formed two asterisms here, and the Arabs knew it as 'the Gazelle with her Young', which is depicted on the Borgian globe (*c.* 1225).
Brightest stars: β LMi, mag 4·4, yellow. 46, mag 3·9, yellow-orange; Hevelius called it *Praecipua*, 'Chief'.
Deep-sky objects: R, LPV, mag range 6·2–13·3, period 372 d, orange-red.

Lepus (Lep)   *The Hare*

A small constellation lying immediately south of Orion and presents a distinctive pattern of stars at approximately the same altitude as Sirius and situated some 20° to the west of it.

In mythology the origin of Lepus is obscure; however, it seems to have some connection with the great devastation wrought in Sicily by hares in early times.
Brightest stars: α Lep *Arneb*, mag 2·7, yellow-white; a giant star with a diameter nine times that of the Sun.

β *Nihal*, mag 3·0, yellow. γ, mag 3·8, yellow-white; also a wide binocular double; mags 3·8 and 6·4, dist 95″; the companion is a striking orange-yellow.
Deep-sky objects: M 79, a globular cluster, mag 8·4, dia 3·2′; just in range with 10 × 50 binoculars as a faint, hazy star.

Libra (Lib)   *The Balance, or Scales*

The seventh sign of the Zodiac and the only inanimate subject included among the twelve signs. For northern observers, most of the constellation is located low in the sky. It is best found by first referring to Antares (α Sco) and then projecting a line towards Arcturus (α Boo).

In mythology it first appears in Greco-Roman folk-lore. An early story associates it with the memory of Mechus, the inventor of weights and measures; a second story associates it with Julius Caesar and a token of his justice; a third story associates it with Astraea, the goddess of justice.
Brightest stars: α Lib, mag 2·9, white; also a fine binocular (optical) double; companion, mag 5·3, yellow-white, dist 230″. β, mag 2·7, blue-white. σ, mag 3·4, an orange-red giant.
Deep-sky objects: Hh 467, a double star, mags 6·9 and 7·7, dist 47″; an object for 2-in telescopes. δ, an Algol-type variable, mag range 4·8–6·2, yellow-white, period 2·3273 d; binocular object.

Microscopium (Mic) *The Microscope*

An inconspicuous Lacaille group with few bright stars. It is formed by neat rectangular borders and is located immediately south of Capricornus, between Piscis Austrinus and Sagittarius.

Brightest stars: α Mic, mag 5, yellow. γ, mag 4·7, yellow. ε, mag 4·8, white; this star was known as 4 PsA before the constellation boundaries were reformed in 1930.

Monoceros (Mon) *The Unicorn*

Although the Milky Way extends across the constellation, it is rather a dull area to the naked eye. It represents another of the modern constellations adopted by Hevelius to fill a large 'vacant' field between Canis Minor and Orion.

Brightest star: α Mon, mag 4·1, yellow-orange.

Deep-sky objects: S, an irregular variable, mag 4·7, greenish-white; a very hot star, but little is known about its light variations. M 50, an open cluster, mag 6·9, dia 16′. NGC 2244, an open cluster, mag 6·2, dia 40′. NGC 2301, an open cluster, mag 5·8, dia 15′. All these clusters can be picked up as hazy objects in binoculars.

Ophiuchus (Oph) *The Serpent Bearer*

A constellation lying exactly in mid heavens, being situated half-way between the north and south poles and the vernal and autumnal equinoxes. Although the ecliptic passes within its southern borders, it is not included among the traditional zodiacal groups. It can be located by extending a line from the Northern Crown to the 1st-magnitude star Altair (α Aql), and half-way along, and a little to the south, is the star Ras Alhague (α Oph).

In mythology Ophiuchus is a serpent bearer and is represented by a giant grasping a writhing serpent (Serpens is a neighbouring constellation). One legend associates the figure with the celebrated physician Aesculapius, son of Apollo.

Brightest stars: α Oph *Ras Alhague,* mag 2·1, white. β *Cebalrai,* mag 2·9, yellow-orange.

Deep-sky objects: X, LPV, mag range 5·9–9·2, period 335 d, orange-red; it can be followed throughout its variations with 12 × 60 binoculars or 2-in telescopes. RS, a recurrent nova (exploding star) which has brightened up on many occasions since its discovery in 1898; mag range 5·3(?)–11·5, period very irregular; its location is well worth keeping under observation since it will likely flare up again in the future. *Note:* the constellation is very rich in globular clusters, six of which can be spotted as nebulous stars with 8 × 30, 10 × 50, or 12 × 60 binoculars (*see* chart for Messier objects M 9, M 10, M 12, M 14, M 19 and M 62).

Orion (Ori) *The Hunter*

One of the most beautiful constellations in the entire heavens and so distinctive that even the most dilatory of stargazers will never forget its configuration once they have seen it.

In mythology, Orion is generally considered to have accompanied Diana and Latone to the chase; he is represented in the sky with a sword suspended from his girdle while attacking the Bull (Taurus, near by) with a huge club held in his right hand. The three bright stars which lie in a straight line, and spaced equidistantly, form the belt or girdle. *Brightest stars:* α Ori *Betelgeuse*, mag 0·7; pronounced bet-el-guz; the name is a corruption from the Arabic *Ibt al Jauzah* meaning 'the Armpit of the Central One'; in the English language its name is often purposely (and humorously) corrupted to 'Beetlejuice'; as a prominent naked-eye star its reddish-orange colour makes it a very conspicuous object. It belongs to the family of Red Giants and has a diameter of 480 million kilometres (300 million miles); in theory the star should just be resolvable as a disc with the 200-in Palomar telescope; but this is *theory* and because of the limitations imposed by the Earth's atmosphere, this is not achieved in practice. It is also an irregular variable star and fluctuates in a mag range 0·3–1·1. β *Rigel*, a brilliant bluish-white star, mag 0·3. γ *Bellatrix*, mag

1·7, blue-white; the ancient astrologers said that all women born under its influence would be lucky and loquacious. δ *Mintaka*, mag 2·5, greenish-white; a belt star. ε *Alnilam*, mag 1·8, greenish-white; the middle star of the belt. ζ *Alnitak*, mag 2·1, blue-white; the southern member of the belt stars. η *Saiph*, mag 3·4, bluish-white; the sword-star of Orion. *Deep-sky objects:* M 42, a gaseous nebula; the famous Great Nebula in Orion (Pl. 7) which is visible in dark, transparent skies to the unaided eye, appearing in the position of θ Orion as a misty star. Even with opera glasses or binoculars a greenish tinge is readily detectable. No photograph can really depict the delicate natural beauty of this glowing cloud of gas which is thought to be the actual birthplace for stars.

Pegasus (Peg) *The Winged Horse*

Easy to recognize because of the 'Square' configuration of four of its brighter members. The star Alpheratz, which forms the north-east corner of the 'Square', is actually borrowed from nearby Andromeda and is common to both groups. Because of its highly distinctive grouping, Pegasus provides a key constellation from which to seek out less arresting neighbouring constellations.

The popular legend involving the Winged Horse is one which involves it with the legend of Perseus's conquest of the Gorgons. To northern observers the head is seen upside down. *Brightest stars:* α Peg *Markab*, mag 2·6, blue-white; an important navigation star. β *Scheat* or *Menkib*, an irregular variable; mag range 2·4–2·8; a red giant ideal for naked-eye study. γ *Algenib*, mag 2·9, blue-white. δ *Alpheratz* (α And), the shared star; mag 2·2, blue-white.

Deep-sky object: M 15, a globular cluster, mag 6·0, dia 7′; it appears as a nebulous star in 8 × 30 binoculars.

Pisces (Psc)   *The Fishes*

The twelfth and last zodiacal sign which lies at the point where the ecliptic, or path of the Sun, crosses the equator in the first part of the year. This point is called the vernal equinox and marks the beginning of the spring season. It is readily located by first searching out the 'Square' of Pegasus and then projecting a line through β and γ Pegasi.

In mythology, Pisces is related to the classic tale of Venus and Cupid who were transformed to fishes by Jupiter so they could escape the giant Typhon. Maps depicting figures of the two fishes always show them with the tails tied together with a cord (*see Pl.* 1).

Brightest stars: α Psc *Al Rischa*, 'the Cord', mag 3·9, white. β *Fum al Samakah*, 'the Fish's Mouth', mag 4·6, blue-white. ρ and 94, a naked-eye pair, mags 5·3 and 5·6, yellow-white and yellow-orange.

Piscis Austrinus (or Australis), (PsA)   *The Southern Fish*

A small constellation south of Aquarius and dominated by the brilliant 1st-magnitude star Fomalhaut.

In legend it shares the same story as the Northern Fishes.

Brightest stars: α PsA *Fomalhaut* or *Fum al Hut*, 'the Fish's Mouth', mag 1·3, white. β, mag 4·4, white.

Deep-sky object: h 5356, a wide double, mags 6 and 7·2, both yellow-white, dist 85″; an easy binocular star.

Puppis (Pup)   *The Stern or Poop*

This group once formed part of the great constellation of Argo Navis which lay mostly in the southern hemisphere and had a total length of 75°. In modern times this great ancient sprawl of stars was divided into four separate constellations: Carina, the Keel; Vela, the Sails; Puppis, the Stern; and Malus, the Mast. This latter group, however, is nowadays represented by Pyxis.

Puppis can be roughly located by projecting a line from Orion's Belt through Sirius and then an equal distance beyond.

The old constellation of Argo was the famous ship which carried Jason and his fifty-four Argonaut companions to Colchis in Thessaly about 1263 B.C., where they ventured after the Golden Fleece.

Note: owing to the constellation becoming a separate entity in modern times, the designations for the brighter members do not follow the usual pattern.

Brightest stars: ζ Pup, mag 2·3, greenish-white. π, mag 2·7, yellow-orange. ρ, mag 2·9, yellow-white.

Deep-sky objects: L², LPV, mag range 3·4–6·2, period 140 d, orange-red; observable through entire range with opera glasses. V, β Lyrae-type eclipsing variable, mag range 4·5–5·2, period 1·4545 d, blue-white. M 46, an open cluster, mag 6·0, dia 24'. M 93, an open cluster, mag 6·0 dia 25'; it includes a wide double, a triple system and two orange-red stars.

Pyxis (Pyx)   *The Mariner's Compass*

A modern group between Puppis and Antlia. It was formed by Lacaille out of the mast of the ancient constellation of Argo. For a time it became obsolete as a separate group, but it was resurrected by the American astronomer Gould when he published his famous work *Uranometria Argentina* in 1879.

Brightest stars: α Pyx, mag 3·7, blue-white. β, mag, 4·0, yellow. γ, mag 4·2, yellow-orange.

Sagitta (Sge)   *The Arrow*

A very inconspicuous group, but it was included as one of the forty-eight constellations of the ancients. It lies south of Cygnus in the plane of the Milky Way, midway between Albireo (β Cyg) and Altair (α Aql). It has no star brighter than the fourth magnitude, and none have recognized Arabic names.

In one legend it represents one of the arrows used by Hercules to kill the vulture which continually gnawed the liver of Prometheus. Another says it is the arrow with which Apollo destroyed the Cyclopes.

Brightest stars: α Sge, mag 4·4, yellow-white. β, mag 4·5, yellow. γ, mag 3·7, orange-yellow. δ, mag 3·8, orange-yellow.

Deep-sky objects: M 71, a globular cluster, mag 8·7, dia 6'; just visible with 12 × 60 binoculars or small telescopes.

Sagittarius (Sgr)   *The Archer*

The ninth constellation of the Zodiac. It lies in the direction of the centre of the Milky Way and is rich in binocular and telescopic objects. It is best located by projecting a line from Deneb (α Cyg) through Altair (α Aql).

Many mythological stories associate Sagittarius with a centaur, a mythical animal which is half horse and half man. A Greek story says that the Centaur is in memory of Chiron, the son of Saturn, who first taught horsemanship. It has been suggested that the Greek name for the Archer is symbolical of sprouting corn, its blades discharged like arrows from the soil. The astrologers of the Middle Ages called it a lucky sign.

Fig. 45   The Lagoon Nebula (M8) in Sagittarius.

Brightest stars: α Sgr *Rukbat*, mag 4·1, blue-white. β^1, β^2 *Arkab* and *Urkab*; a wide naked-eye (optical) double; mags 4·3 and 4·5, blue-white, white; β^1 is a telescopic double, mags 4·3 and 7·1, dist 28″. γ *Al Nasl*, mag 3·1, yellow. δ *Media*, mag 2·8, yellow. ε *Kaus Australis*, mag 1·9, blue-white. λ *Kaus Borealis*, mag 2·9, yellow.

Deep-sky objects: 54, a double for 2-in telescopes; mags 6·0 and 7·5, dist 45″, yellow and blue. W, a Cepheid-type variable, mag range 4·8–6·0, period 7·5947 d. X, a Cepheid-type variable, mag range 5·0–6·1, period 7·0122 d. AQ, an irregular variable, mag range 6·6–7·6, brilliant red; red tint is very noticeable in binoculars. *Note:* There are more than 15 Messier objects in this constellation, all of which are visible in small telescopes, and 12 with binoculars including: M 8, a gaseous nebula, 'the Lagoon Nebula', so named due to its appearance in photographs (Fig. 45); mag 6·8, size 60′ × 35′. M 17, a gaseous nebula, 'the Omega Nebula'; so named owing to its unique appearance in long exposure photographs when it resembles the Greek letter Ω, mag 7·0 size 46′ × 37′ (*see* also charts).

Scorpius (Sco)   *The Scorpion*

The eighth sign of the Zodiac, one can easily imagine the scorpion from the chance configuration of its brightest stars. It lies due south of Ophiuchus, with Sagittarius and Libra on either side. Its principal star, Antares, dominates a compact group of stars, six of which are brighter than the 3rd magnitude.

In mythology it has been represented by different symbols including a snake or a crocodile, but more commonly it is a scorpion. It supposedly is the animal which killed Orion at the command of Juno. In Roman times, when a comet passed over the constellation, it was supposed to portend a plague of reptiles or insects.

Brightest stars: α Sco *Antares*, 'the Rival of Mars'—a name given because of its brilliant, fiery reddish hue, and because it lies close to the ecliptic and the two are often in close proximity; this star is a red supergiant over 590 million kilometres in diameter; mag 1·2. β *Graffias* or *Grappine*, mag 2·0. δ *Dschubba*, mag 2·5, blue. ζ^1, ζ^2, mags 4·9 and 3·7, blue and orange; a wide optical double for opera glasses or binoculars. λ, mag 1·7, blue. μ^1, μ^2, mags 3·1 and 3·6, both blue; naked-eye pair.

Deep-sky objects: ω^1, ω^2; a wide naked-eye pair just south of β Sco; mags 4·1 and 4·6, blue and yellow. RR, LPV, mag range 5·0–12·2, period 279·5 d, orange-red; this star lies in the same field as M 62, a globular cluster lying just over the border in Ophiuchus; mag 6·6. *Note:* Scorpio is extremely rich in star clusters, several of which can be seen through binoculars or small telescopes (*see* charts).

Sculptor (Scl) *The Sculptor*

Another inconspicuous Lacaille group formed by stars between Cetus and Phoenix. It is best found by first locating the bright star Fomalhaut (α PsA); and Sculptor lies immediately to its west. Although a southern constellation, it can be seen from latitude 40° N.

To the naked eye it is a sparse constellation, but it swarms with clusters of extragalactic nebulae, some of which can be seen with moderate-sized telescopes.

Brightest stars: α Scl, mag 4·4, blue-white. β, mag 4·5, blue-white. γ, mag 4·5, yellow. δ, mag 4·6, white. *Deep-sky objects:* NGC 253, a galaxy appearing 'edge-on'; mag 7·5, size 20′ × 6′; well seen in 2-in telescopes and just visible in coal-black, transparent skies with binoculars. NGC 55, another galaxy appearing edge-on, mag 8, size 25′ × 3′; an object for 2-in telescopes.

Scutum (Sobieskii) (Sct) *Sobieski's Shield*

Formed by Hevelius in the seventeenth century from seven unformed 4th-magnitude stars between Serpens Cauda, Aquila and Sagittarius, in honour of John III Sobieski, King of Poland.

The principal stars are intended to represent the coat of arms of the

house of Sobieski. When the Polish king was victorious against the Turks in 1683, the sign of the cross was emblazoned on his shield to commemorate his heroic deeds.
Brightest stars: α Sct, mag 4·1, yellow-orange. β, mag 4·5, yellow. γ, mag 4·7, white.
Deep-sky objects: R Sct, RV Tauri-type variable, mag range 4·7–7·8, period 144 d, yellow-orange; ideal for binocular study. M 11, a compact cluster, mag 6·3, dia 10′; fan-shaped with a bright star at apex; a splendid binocular object. *Note:* Several exploding stars (novae) have been discovered within the boundaries of Scutum by amateur astronomers; a recent one was in 1970.

Serpens (Ser) *The Serpent*

In the past it was often grouped with Ophiuchus. Nowadays Serpens is divided into two parts, Serpens Cauda and Serpens Caput, lying either side of Ophiuchus.

In Greek folk-lore, both Ophiuchus and Serpens symbolized Aesculapius, the ship's doctor of the Argonauts' voyage in search of the Golden Fleece. By watching a serpent, Aesculapius learnt the secret of a magic herb which he later used to treat the sick.
Brightest stars: (Serpens Caput) α Ser *Unukalhai*, mag 2·7, yellow-orange. β, mag 3·0, blue; the Chinese knew it by the name of 'Chow'.
Brightest stars: (Serpens Cauda) ζ Ser,

mag 4·6, yellow-white. ε, mag 3·6, white.
Deep-sky objects: (Serpens Caput) M 5, a globular cluster, mag 6·2, dia 12′; well seen in binoculars and in small telescopes; an old friend to 'comet-sweepers' when it is located in the morning sky.
Deep-sky objects: (Serpens Cauda) M16, an open star cluster, mag 6·4, dia 25′; quite noticeable in 8 × 30 binoculars.

Sextans (Sex) *The Sextant*

A dull-looking group to the naked eye, but long-exposure photographs show the whole area to be strewn with galaxies. It is best located from the Leo 'sickle', since it lies due south of Regulus (α Leo).

This is another of Hevelius's modern constellations, formed in 1680 to commemorate either the sextant used by the Englishman Hadley in 1730 or the earlier sextant used by the Danish nobleman Tycho Brahe, who was the last great pre-telescopic observer.
Brightest stars: α Sex, mag 4·5, white. β, mag 4·9, blue-white.

Taurus (Tau) *The Bull*

The second of the twelve signs of the Zodiac; it depicted the vernal (Spring) equinox from about 4000 B.C. to 1700 B.C. Although the Pleiades star cluster now is included as part of this constellation, in ancient times it was often reckoned as a separate one. Taurus can be located immediately south of Auriga (sharing one of its stars) and north and west of Orion.

The Bull is one of the oldest constellations and in Greek mythology is the sign which commemorates the animal which bore Europa safely across the sea to Crete. The five brightest stars which form the Hyades cluster are reputed to represent five of the twelve daughters of Atlas, King of Mauretania, and his wife, Pleione. Their names were Phaola, Ambrosia, Eudora, Coronis and Polyxo. The Pleiades cluster represents the other seven daughters of Atlas, sisters to the Hyades. Their names were Alcyone, Merope, Maya, Electra, Taygete, Sterope and Celaeno. Legend says that Merope was the only sister who married a mortal, and it is on this account that the star is fainter than the rest.

Brightest stars: α Tau *Aldebaran*, 'the Follower' or 'the Hindmost' because it follows the Pleiades in their journey round the heavens; mag 1·1, yellow-orange. β *El Nath*, mag 1·8, blue-white; a star shared with neighbouring Auriga (identical with γ Aurigae). γ

Hyadum I or *Prima Hyadum*, mag 3·9, yellow; located at the apex of the V-shape forming the Hyades cluster. ε, mag 3·6, yellow; Flamsteed called it Oculus boreus, 'the Northern Eye'.

Hyades: This so-called open cluster involves many of the brighter stars forming the group depicted like a capital V turned on its side. Aldebaran marks the upper left hand, ε the right-hand side and γ the apex.

Pleiades: No other group of stars figures so largely in myth and legend. Although they are known as 'the Seven Sisters', with ordinary eyes only six will be readily counted, but observers with good eyesight have claimed to have counted up to fourteen when the sky is particularly transparent. With binoculars and small telescopes the cluster is beautifully resolved into many stars (*see* Fig. 46 and Pl. 6.)

Deep-sky objects: σ¹, σ², mags 5·2 and 4·9, both white; a wide naked-eye pair 7′ dist; best seen in opera glasses or binoculars. M 1, a planetary nebula, the famous Crab Nebula (Pl. 3) mag 8·4, size 6′ × 4′; in a really

Fig. 46 The Pleiades open star cluster (M45).

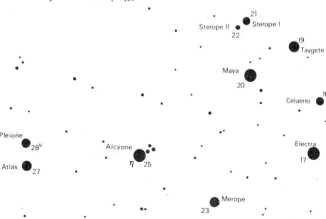

transparent sky it is just seen with 8 × 30s. This nebula is now known to be the result of a spectacular supernova explosion which was recorded in Chinese and Japanese chronicles of A.D. 1054. It also contains the first pulsar to be detected visually. Pulsars are probably neutron stars whose material is so densely packed that they give rise to bizarre physical phenomena difficult to fit into the framework of the known laws of physics.

Triangulum (Tri)   *The Triangle*
The group lies south-east of Andromeda, north of Aries and west of Perseus. In the past the constellation figure was represented by two triangles, but nowadays the smaller triangle is no longer recognized.
Brightest stars: α Tri *Caput Trianguli*, mag 3·6, yellow-white. β, mag 3·1, white. γ, mag 4·1, white.
Deep-sky object: M 33, a spiral galaxy, mag 6·7, size 60′ × 40′; one of the nearest galaxies at a distance of 200 million light years; it is best observed with low magnification and is well seen in 8 × 30 binoculars as a comparatively large, faint haze, but the eye must first be fully adapted to night vision.

Virgo (Vir)   *The Virgin*
The sixth sign of the Zodiac. An extremely long constellation bounded on the east by Libra and on the west by Leo. In April its sprawling con-figuration straddles the meridian at midnight.

Virgo is dominated by the 1st-magnitude star Spica, which traditionally marks the ear of wheat in the Virgin's left hand. It forms a striking equilateral triangle with Arcturus (α Boo) and Denebola (α Leo).

In mythology one story associates it with Justitia who, while she lived on Earth in the golden age, taught mankind their duty. Another story relates it to Ceres, who holds the ear of corn (*see* above) in her hand. According to Pliny, the appearance of a comet within the borders of Virgo signified to the Roman astrologers grievous ills to all females.
Brightest stars: α Vir *Spica*, mag 1·2, blue-white; one of the brightest stars in the sky and well known to navigators as a lunar star, as it is situated 2° south of the ecliptic. Some believe several Greek temples were orientated towards it. It was a very important calendar star to the Megalithic astronomers of North West Europe in about 2000 B.C. β *Zavijava* or *Zarijan*, mag 3·8, yellow-white. γ *Porrima*, mag 2·7, yellow-white; it was named by some of the ancients as the goddess of prophecy, sister of Carmenta, worshipped by women. δ, mag 3·6; orange-red giant star over 700 times more luminous than the Sun.
Deep-sky objects: R Vir, LPV, mag range 6·2–12·6, period 145 d, orange-red. *Note:* there are many telescopic galaxies within the borders of Virgo,

at least 11 of which are visible in 3-in telescopes (*see* chart).

Vulpecula (Vul) *The Little Fox* (*and Goose*)

One of the least conspicuous and least known star configurations in the northern heavens. However, it is easily located owing to its close proximity to the more prominent groups of Cygnus and Aquila; it lies about half-way between Deneb (α Cyg) and Altair (α Aql).

Vulpecula is a modern constellation arranged by Hevelius out of unformed stars of the ancients. Hevelius actually formed two constellations 'the Fox' and 'the Goose', but in modern times the Goose is generally omitted.

Brightest star: α Vul (*Anser?*), mag 4·6, orange-red.

Deep-sky objects: M 27, the famous 'Dumb-bell Nebula' (Pl. 5) so called because of its telescopic appearance; it is a planetary nebula whose form is readily seen with 8 × 30 binoculars. NGC 6940, an open star cluster, mag 8·2, dia 20′; it can just be detected with binoculars (using averted vision, *see* p. 35) in a dark, very transparent sky.

Southern Constellations

Apus (Aps)   *The Bird of Paradise*

A group of southern stars lying about 13° from the southern celestial pole; situated immediately below the Southern Triangle (TrA). It was introduced on to star maps by Johann Bayer in the seventeenth century, but several believe its invention belongs to Petrus Theodorus (Pieter Dirckszoon Keyser) the early sixteenth-century Dutch navigator.

Brightest stars: α Aps, mag 3·8, yellow-orange. β, mag 4·2, yellow. γ, mag 3·9, yellow-orange.

Deep-sky objects: δ¹, δ², a wide binocular double, mags 4·8 and 5·2; both cool orange-red stars. θ, a semiregular variable, mag range 6·4–8·6, orange-red.

Ara (Ara)   *The Altar*

One of the original forty-eight constellations of the Greeks which Ptolemy called 'the Censor'. Located between Scorpius and α Triangulum Australe on the edge of the Milky Way. Aratus in his classic poem *Phenomena* directs: 'Below the fiery sting of the dread monster, Scorpion, and near the south is hung the Altar.'

In mythology, Ara was the altar on which the gods swore when Zeus proceeded against Cronus.

Brightest stars: α Ara, mag 3·0, blue-white; in ancient China it was called Choo, a club or staff. β, mag 2·8,

yellow-orange. γ, mag 3·5, blue-white. δ, mag 3·8, blue-white. ζ, mag 3·1, yellow-orange.

Deep-sky objects: R, an Algol-type variable, mag range 6·0–7·0, blue-white, period 4·42 d. NGC 6193, an open cluster, mag 5·0, dia 20′; an easy binocular object. NGC 6167, an open cluster, mag 6·4, dia 18′; appears as a nebulous star in binoculars. NGC 6397, a globular cluster, mag 4·7, dia 20′; a glorious bright object.

Carina (Car)   *The Keel (of Argo Navis)*

A large southern constellation which once formed part of the ancient group of Argo Navis. It contains the star Canopus second only in brightness to Sirius. Canopus in contemporary times is a star frequently chosen as a primary navigation star for space vehicles despatched as interplanetary probes. The whole constellation is rich in interesting bright objects, including many star clusters (*see* below and charts).

In mythology Carina formed the keel of the famous ship Argo Navis (*see* p. 98).

Brightest stars: α Car *Canopus*, mag −0·9, a super yellow-white giant; the star was named after the famous chief pilot of the fleet of Menelaos; when he died in Egypt on the return voyage from Troy, a town was named after him (now in ruins on the site of a village known as Aboukir). It was in this town that Ptolemy made his observations of the heavens. β *Miaplacidus*, mag 1·8, white. ε, mag 1·7, yellow-orange. θ, mag 3·0, blue-white. ι *Tureis*, mag 2·3, yellow-white.

Deep-sky objects: R, LPV, mag range 4·0–11·1, period 309·15 d, orange-red. S, LPV, mag range 5·5–8·8, period 149·4 d, orange-red; the area round about this star is strewn with glorious star fields. NGC 3532, a brilliant open cluster, mag 3·3, dia 60′; visible to the naked eye as a hazy patch of light and a magnificent spectacle in binoculars. NGC 2516, bright open cluster, mag 3·0, dia 60′; much like Praesepe and clearly visible to the naked eye. θ Car (I.2602), a bright naked-eye cluster reminiscent of the Pleiades; mag 1·6, dia 70′; the group consists of over 30 stars forming a memorable sight in binoculars. η Car, a peculiar irregular variable which brightened to mag −1 in 1843 and for a time outshone Canopus; by 1880 it had faded to mag 7·0 and since then it has continued to fluctuate up and down. It should be watched carefully by all southern hemsiphere star spotters in the event it should suddenly increase in brilliance. Around this star is a great diffuse nebula visible in binoculars, and the whole area is so richly adorned it is almost beyond literal description: there are brilliant star groupings contrasting with dark, black obscuring clouds, one known as 'the Key Hole' owing to its suggestive outline. One of the most rewarding pursuits for southern stargazers is to lie back relaxed in a garden chair and sweep this whole glorious area with binoculars.

Chamaeleon (Cha)   *The Chameleon*

A small, modern southern constellation located between Carina and the south celestial pole. It was formed by Bayer in 1604 from observations gleaned from voyagers to the southern hemisphere. In ancient China part of the group was known as Seaou Tow—a small dipper.

Brightest stars: α Cha, mag 4·1, yellowish-white. β, mag 4·1, orange-red. δ¹ and δ², mags 5·5 and 4·6, yellow and white; a wide binocular double.

Circinus (Cir)   *The Pair of Compasses*

One of Lacaille's new constellations between Centaurus and the Southern Triangle and lying in the plane of the Milky Way.

Brightest star: α Cir, mag 3·4, yellowish white.

Corona Australis (CrA)   *The Southern Crown*

A small, inconspicuous constellation between Sagittarius and Scorpius. Although situated well south, it was a group included among the original forty-eight constellations of Ptolemy.

Bayer in his star map depicted Corona as a typical wreath but lacking the streaming ribbons of its northern namesake.

Brightest stars: α CrA, mag 4·1, a hot white star. β, mag 4·2, yellow. γ, mag 4·3, yellow-white. δ, mag 4·7, yellow-orange.

Deep-sky object: NGC 6541, a globular cluster, mag 5·8, dia 6′; an object well within binocular range.

Crux (Cru) *The Southern Cross*

Although quite a small constellation, Crux Australis is a group of universal interest to all stargazers. In the southern hemisphere it never fails to command the attention—and the poetic and literary fancies—of first-time travellers to these climes. As it lies directly in the plane of the Milky Way, it contains many attractive objects, including ten bright open clusters. For northern observers it begins to hove into view in the latitude of Florida. Owing to the effects of precession, 5,000 years back it was visible from the shores of the Baltic Sea, and one day in the distant future it will re-emerge above the northern European horizon.

The Southern Cross is symbolized on the Australian national flag—first raised near Ballarat in 1854 when incensed gold miners defied unjust government mining laws. The Southern Cross was seen by the early navigators as a symbol of Christian faith, and in its present form it is

Fig. 47   Aboriginal bark painting depicting the Southern Cross and the pointers of Centaurus. See p. 149.

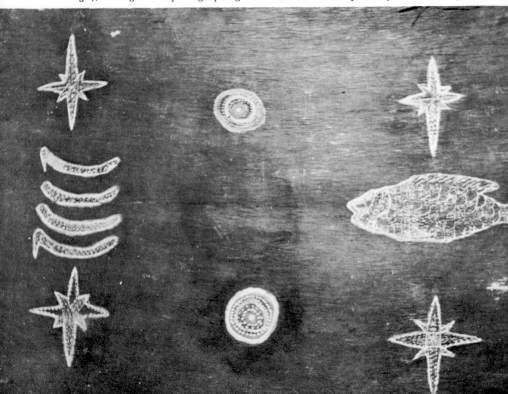

Fig. 48   The Southern Cross and the Coal Sack.

attributed to the invention of Royer in 1679, but it was well known to Europeans as a distinct group two centuries before this time. In the fifteenth century it was frequently alluded to as 'the Southern Celestial Clock', since with a little familiarity and regard for the degree of 'uprightness' of the cross, one can readily tell the time of night (*see* p. 141). γ and α can be used in the fashion of the Pointers of Ursa Major to indicate the approximate position of the south pole—about 27½° distant from α.

The Polynesians and Aborigines had many legends about it, and it is frequently depicted on contemporary Aboriginal bark paintings (Fig. 47).

Brightest stars: α Cru, mag 1·1; a double for 2-in telescopes; mags 1·6 and 2·1, dist 4·4″, both blue-white. One tribe of Aborigines called it *Yukope*, 'the Green Parroquet'. β, mag 1·5, blue-white; the Aborigines called it *Dantum*, 'Blue-mountain Parrot'. γ, mag 1·6, brilliant orange-red. δ, mag 3·1, blue-white; it has a wide binocular companion, dist 2′, white.

Deep-sky objects: 'The Coal Sack'; a large patch of interstellar gas and dust *c.* 7° × 4° which obscures the background stars of the Milky Way lying beyond it; in wide-angle binoculars the whole area presents a glorious spectacle (Fig. 48). NGC 4755, an open cluster, mag 5·2, dia 10′; it can just be glimpsed with the naked eye next to β on a really dark night.

Fig. 49   The Great Magellanic Cloud (Nubecula Major).

Dorado (Dor)   *The Swordfish*

A group between Reticulum and Pictor introduced by Bayer in 1604. It contains the interesting naked-eye galaxy Nubecula Major, or the Greater Magellanic Cloud, which it shares with near-by Mensa. It was named after Ferdinand Magellan who set out to circumnavigate the globe in 1519; this cloud contains S Doradus, the most luminous star known, estimated to be about 400,000 times brighter than the Sun.

Dorado is often referred to as 'the Goldfish'; but now it is associated with the swordfish; although it should actually, under the name Dorado (from the Spanish), refer to the common dolphin (*Coryphaena hippurus*) which in life is one of most beautifully coloured cosmopolitan fishes in the ocean.

Brightest stars: α Dor, mag 3·5, white. β, a Cepheid-type variable, mag range 4·5–5·8, period 9·84 d, yellowish-white. γ, mag 4·4, yellow-white. δ, mag 4·5, white.

Deep-sky objects: Nubecula Major, the Greater (or Larger) Magellanic Cloud; together with *Nubecula Minor* they are known as the Cape Clouds, both prominent naked-eye objects. In Australia, during the colonial days, they were often referred to as 'the Drover's Friends', since they were utilized by drovers as directional aids when cattle were moved in the cool of night. They still provide an excellent directional aid to modern travellers in remote Outback locales or in dense bushland. Both clouds are vast, independent stellar systems and 'close' neighbours to our own Milky Way; the larger cloud is 150,000 light-years distant. R, a semi-regular variable, mag range 4·8–6·8, period 338 d, orange-crimson.

Grus (Gru)   *The Crane*

A southern constellation formed by Bayer in 1604. Located between Indus and Phoenix and lying south of the bright star Fomalhaut (α PsA).
Brightest stars: α Gru *Alnair*, 'the Bright One', mag 2·2, blue-white. β, mag 2·2, orange-red. γ, mag 3·6, blue-white. δ^1, δ^2, a wide naked-eye optical double;mags 4·0 and 4·3, yellow and orange-red.
Deep-sky objects: π, a wide (optical) binocular double; π^1, an irregular variable of very deep red; mag range 5·8–6·4; π^2, mag 5·8, yellow-white, dist 3'.

Horologium (Hor)   *The Pendulum Clock*

An inconspicuous constellation whose principal stars are faint; it was formed by Lacaille. Located between the most southern portion of Eridanus and the groups Caelum, Dorado and Reticulum. Not far away is the brilliant star Achernar (α Eri).
Brightest stars: α Hor, mag 3·8, yellow-orange. β, mag 5·1, white.

Hydrus (Hyi)   *The Sea Serpent* (or *Water Snake*)

A Bayer constellation between Horologium and Tucana and the Greater and Lesser Magellanic Clouds. Julius Schiller, who reformed the constellations into biblical figures, called it Raphael. To the ancient Chinese it was also a sea serpent.
Brightest stars: α Hyi, mag 3·0, white. β, mag 3·8, yellow. γ, mag 3·2, orange-red.

Indus (Ind)   *The Indian*

An inconspicuous southern group lying between Grus and Pavo. It was originated by Bayer on the assumption that its configuration represents a typical North American Indian completely naked but with arrows in both hands. Later depictions give the figure a spear in his right hand (Pl. 1).
Brightest stars: α Ind, mag 3·2, yellow. β, mag 3·7, yellow-orange. δ, mag 4·6, yellow.
Deep-sky object: θ, a double suitable for 2-in telescopes; mags 4·6 and 7·2, dist 6", white.

Lupus (Lup)   *The Wolf*

A group lying between Centaurus and Scorpius in a rich region of the sky, encompassing part of the Milky Way. It was known to the Greeks and Romans simply as the Wild Animal, but it was recognized as a separate group long before this.

In mythology it is the wolf into which Lycaon, King of Arcadia, was changed on account of his cruelty.
Brightest stars: α Lup, mag 2·9, blue-white; in China it was called Yang

Mun or Men, the South Gate. β, mag 2·8, blue-white. γ, mag 3·0, blue-white.

Deep-sky object: NGC 5822, an open cluster, mag 6·4, dia 40′; a cluster formed by about 120 stars; an ideal binocular subject.

Mensa (Men)   *The Table Mountain*

A group originally called Mons Mensae and formed by the French astronomer Lacaille to perpetuate the memory of his sojourn in South Africa where in 1751–1752 he stayed to survey the southern heavens. Poor Lacaille was never to see the fruits of his labours, for he died in 1762; his friend Maraldi published the results of his work the following year. The constellation supposedly represents the mountain behind Cape Town which had been witness to his nightly vigils.

The group is situated near the southern pole just north of Octans, and although a dull, faint area, it includes part of the rich Greater Magellanic Cloud (Nubecula Major), which overlaps from neighbouring Dorado.

Brightest stars: α Men, mag 5·1, yellow-orange. β, mag 5·3, yellow.

Musca (Mus)   *The Southern Fly*

A small constellation lying just south of Crux and containing some fine telescopic objects. Introduced by Bayer as Apis, the Bee, but Lacaille changed its designation to the present one in 1752. In Julius Schiller's biblical constellations, together with Apus and Chamaeleon, it depicted mother Eve.

Brightest stars: α Mus, mag 2·9, blue-white. β, mag 3·3, blue-white. γ, mag 4·0, blue-white. δ, mag 3·6, yellow-orange.

Deep-sky objects: NGC 4833, a globular cluster visible with binoculars as a hazy star; mag 7·0, dia 5′. NGC 4372, globular cluster just visible in 2-in telescopes; mag 8, dia 12′. BO, an irregular variable, mag range 6·0–6·7, orange-red; it is located at the apex of an equilateral triangle formed by BO and α and β.

Norma (Nor)   *The Level and Square*

A constellation reconstructed by Lacaille to its present form from earlier star configurations of Theodorus and Bayer who called it the Southern Triangle. It lies adjacent and south of Scorpio in a rich part of the sky—well worth sweeping with binoculars—but it is a difficult constellation to trace out with the naked eye. Owing to the rearrangement of the constellation boundaries in 1930, Lacaille's α star is now in another group.

Brightest stars: γ^2 Nor, mag 4·1, yellow. γ^1, mag 5·0, a yellow supergiant. δ, mag 4·8, white. ϵ, mag 4·8, blue-white.

Deep-sky objects: NGC 6067, an open cluster, mag 6·7, dia 15′. NGC 6087, an open cluster, mag 6·0, dia 20′. Both clusters are visible as hazy, silvery patches in binoculars.

Octans (Oct)   *The Octant*

A group occupying a barren region round the southern celestial pole. It contains the nearest star to the pole visible to the naked eye, σ Octanis, mag 5·5, which lies about 1° away from the exact polar position. The group was formed by Lacaille in 1752 to commemorate the instrument invented by John Hadley in 1730.

Brightest stars: α Oct, mag 5·2, yellowish-white; one of the faintest designated Alpha stars in the entire heavens. β, mag 4·3, yellowish-white. δ, mag 4·1, yellow-orange.

Pavo (Pav)   *The Peacock*

One of Bayer's twelve invented southern constellations, located between Telescopium and Octans. Although a modern group, the title 'Peacock' is appropriate in its mythological context, since in early times it was a symbol of immortality and has been associated with Juno, the immortal queen of the heavens, and Argos, the builder of the ship Argo, who was changed by Juno to a peacock when his great vessel was transferred to the sky.

Brightest stars: α Pav, mag 2·1, blue-white. β, mag 3·6, white. γ, mag 4·3, yellowish white. δ, mag 3·6, yellow. *Deep-sky objects:* κ, a Cepheid-type variable, mag range 4·0–5·5, period 9·0838d, yellowish-white. ε, a double for 2-in telescopes; mags 4·2 and 8·1, dist 3·5″; bright orange-red and white

providing a wonderful colour contrast. NGC 6752, a globular cluster, mag 5·0, dia 13′; very easy with binoculars and has been called 'one of the gems of the southern skies'.

Phoenix (Phe)   *The Phoenix*

Located between Eridanus and Grus, south of Fornax and Sculptor. It was introduced by Bayer, but it originally

Fig. 50   The Ikeya-Seki Sungrazing comet.

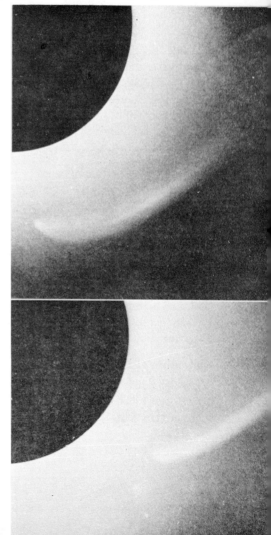

represented a boat and later a figure of young ostriches. Later it was changed into a griffin or eagle and finally became the mythical bird which rose again from its own ashes after destruction by fire.

To the ancient Egyptians, the Phoenix as Bennu, symbolized immortality, and in the sky it symbolized the brilliant Sungrazer comets which skim so close to the Sun's surface at perihelion that they appear to be swallowed up and destroyed. But in spite of their close approach, these comets survive and then retreat back into the depths of space half-way towards the nearest stars. The famous Ikeya-Seki Comet in 1965 (Fig. 50) was such an example (*see* also p. 123). *Brightest stars:* α Phe, mag 2·4, yellow. β, mag 3·4, yellow. γ, mag 3·4, orange-red. δ, mag 4·0, yellow.

Pictor (Pic)   *The Painter's Easel*

A small group lying south of Columba and near Canopus (α Car). Formerly it was called Equuleus Pictoris, a group formed by Lacaille.
Brightest stars: α Pic, mag 3·3, white, near by lies the nebulous remnants of the faint 12th mag star which exploded to become Nova Pictoris 1925 and reached a brightness of mag 1·1 at maximum.

Reticulum (Ret)   *The Net*

A Lacaille rearrangement of an earlier constellation called Rhombus, invented by Isaak Habrecht. It supposedly represents the reticle which was used by Lacaille to assist him map out the stars of the southern hemisphere. The group lies between Dorado and Horologium and not far distant from Nubecula Major (the Greater Magellanic Cloud).
Brightest stars: α Ret, mag 3·4, yellow. β, mag 3·8, yellow. γ, mag 4·5, orange-red. ζ¹ and ζ², mags 5·5 and 5·2, both yellow; a wide (optical) binocular double.

Telescopium (Tel)   *The Telescope*

A configuration formed by Lacaille from a small, insignificant star grouping situated between Pavo and Sagittarius. This constellation should not be confused with the now obsolete group Telescopium Herschelii, between Lynx and Gemini, formed by the Abbé Hell in 1781 in honour of Sir William Herschel.
Brightest stars: α Tel, mag 3·8, blue-white. δ¹, δ², mags 5·1 and 5·3, both blue-white; a wide (optical) binocular double. ε, mag 4·6, yellow. ξ, mag 4·1, yellow-orange.

Triangulum Australis (TrA)   *The Southern Triangle*

A group lying between Ara and Circinus and quickly located owing to its proximity to the bright star α Cen (lying immediately to the east of the group). It is the southern equivalent of the Northern Triangle, but it is a more prominent configuration. It first appeared in the star maps of Bayer, who borrowed it from Petrus Theodorus of a century earlier.

Brightest stars: α TrA, mag 1·9, yellow-orange. β, mag 3·0, yellow-white. γ, mag 3·1, white.

Deep-sky objects: NGC 6025, an open cluster, mag 5·8, dia 10′; a group formed by about 30 stars and easy to spot with binoculars.

Tucana (Tuc)   *The Toucan*

A Bayer constellation lying south of Phoenix and previously called 'the American Goose'. It contains the Lesser Magellanic Cloud (Nubecula Minor), an irregular galaxy and one of the closest to the Milky Way at a distance of 165,000 light-years. The

old navigators often termed both the Larger and Lesser Magellanic Clouds the Cape Clouds.

Brightest stars: α Tuc, mag 2·9, yellow-orange. β¹ and β², a wide double; mags 4·5 and 4·5, both blue-white. δ, mag 4·8, blue-white.

Deep-sky objects: The Lesser Magellanic Cloud; a companion to our own galaxy; in the southern hemisphere it remains a circumpolar object throughout the night. Within the cloud are many objects such as clusters and gaseous nebulae, some of which are resolvable with comparatively little optical aid. NGC 104, a bright globular cluster visible to the naked eye as a 5th mag star 47 Tuc; a wonderful

Fig. 51   The Small Magellanic Cloud (Nubecula Minor).

object in binoculars; dia 23′. NGC 362, a globular cluster, mag 6·8, dia 5′; visible as a hazy star in binoculars.

Vela (Vel)   *The Sail*

Located north of Carina between Puppis and Centaurus. Another of the three groups which were part of the division of Argo Navis when the ancient constellation was split up. It lies in the plane of the Milky Way and contains a number of irregular banded clouds of absorbing dust. These have the effect of blotting out the stars lying behind them, giving the appearance of holes in the sky, to which the name 'coal-sack' is often descriptively applied.
Brightest stars: γ^1, γ^2 Vel, a four-star group; γ^1, mag 4·8, blue-white; γ^2, mag 2·2, greenish-white, dist 41″; γ^{1-2} are fine objects in 2-in telescopes. δ, mag 2·0, white. λ *Alsuhail*, mag 2·2, a yellow-orange supergiant. μ, mag 2·8, yellow. κ, mag 2·6, blue-white.

Deep-sky objects: NGC 3228, an open cluster, mag 6·5, dia 30′. H3 and I.2391, adjoining open clusters, very bright and clearly visible in binoculars. NGC 2547, an open cluster, mag 5·1, dia 15′; an aggregation of about 50 stars beautifully shown by binoculars. I.2395, a loose open cluster mag 4·6, dia 10′.

Volans (Vol)   *The Flying Fish*

A group lying between the Larger Magellanic Cloud and Carina. It is another of Bayer's asterisms and was formerly entitled Piscis Volans.
Brightest stars: α Vol, mag 4·2, white. β, mag 3·7, yellow-orange. γ^1, mag 5·8, yellow. γ^2, mag 3·9, yellow-white. δ, mag 4·0, yellow-white.
Deep-sky objects: ζ, a very colourful double, mags 3·9 and 9·0, dist 17″, orange and white. ϵ, a double system; mags 4·5 and 8·0, dist 6″, both blue-white. Both these objects are ideal subjects for 2-in telescopes.

Planet Spotting

THE Greeks called the planets wanderers, and the name planet is derived from the Greek *planetes*, meaning 'wanderer'. Five are plainly visible from time to time with the naked eye: Mercury, Venus, Mars, Jupiter and Saturn. Long before their true natures were recognized, all these planets were well known to the ancient races as 'stars' which moved.

The fundamental difference between a planet and a star is one of physical characteristics. The stars, like our own Sun (which is a typical average star) are self-luminous gaseous bodies, and we see them as a consequence of their own radiation. The planets, however, are cool, non-luminous bodies that generate insufficient energy within their interiors to render them visible in ordinary wavelengths of light. We see planets only by the light reflected back off their surfaces or atmospheres, which first reaches them from the Sun.

Although this simple definition of stars and planets holds good for objects in nearer space, elsewhere in the Universe there may be bizarre objects which do not fit into either of these familiar categories.

From our position on Earth all the planets appear to move across the sky confined to the zodiacal constellations. This is because all the planets revolve round the Sun in orbits approximately in the same plane with the exception of some of the asteroids, or minor planets, whose orbits are steeply inclined. Since the Earth's axis is tilted at $23\frac{1}{2}°$, this plane, or the *ecliptic*, also appears to be tilted in relation to the celestial equator, and they only coincide at the time of the equinoxes (*see* Fig. 11c).

When the star spotter has familiarized himself with the general pattern of the constellations, or perhaps when he is in the very act of identifying their brightest stars, a stranger may be noted which is not shown on the star charts. First reaction might be a quickening of the blood with the thought that a nova, or 'new' star, has been spotted. Of course, it may well be that a nova has been found, just as other amateur observers have found novae in the past. Nevertheless, before jumping to conclusions, it must be remembered that the chances are that it is some other well-known transient object such as a planet. This can easily be verified by using the planet tables (*see* below).

Genuine novae, or other new discoveries such as comets, are reported to the Central Bureau for Astronomical Telegrams at present located in Cambridge, Mass, USA. However, new objects are first reported to the National Observatory of the country in which the observer is living, so that they can first be confirmed as genuine discoveries. Apart from genuine reports, observatories receive numerous reports of pseudo-discoveries which in many instances turn out to be observations of well-known bright planets, in particular Venus and Jupiter.

Planet Spotting Tables

At the end of this section is a set of planet tables for the period 1981–1993 which are especially designed for amateur star and planet spotters who otherwise have no up-to-date information about the positions of the planets visible to the naked eye. By the use of these tables and the charts on pp. 48–67 (or key maps pp. 39–45) the planet spotter can locate, at any time, the positions in the sky of any of the brighter planets and their angular separations from the Sun. If an observer wishes to make a planet identification, or if a bright stranger is seen in a star field, the information can be gleaned from the appropriate column in a matter of seconds and plotted on the charts or maps *lightly in pencil*.

Observing the Planets

Even to a casual observer, the brighter planets are noticeably different in appearance from the fixed stars. They appear to shine with a much steadier light, and the effect is a real one. The stars twinkle, or scintillate, because they are so far distant from the Earth that their light can be reckoned as an extremely narrow point source. The planets, on the other hand, are much closer, and although we cannot see their discs with the naked eye, their larger apparent diameters make their images less susceptible to displacement when passing through the ever-turbulent atmosphere of the Earth.

In addition to our own Earth there are eight major planets in the solar system, three of which—Uranus, Neptune and Pluto—were discovered by the aid of the telescope. Apart from the major planets there are thousands of asteroids, or minor planets, which are chiefly concentrated between the orbits of Mars and Jupiter. Several asteroids have eccentric orbits like those of the comets, and during the history of the Earth, some have fallen as meteorites and have gouged out sizable craters.

Mercury

Mercury has a diameter of 4,840 km and revolves round the Sun in 88 days.

Since it lies within the Earth's orbit, it can only be seen with the naked eye shortly after sunset as an evening 'star', or as a morning 'star' before dawn, depending where the planet is located in its orbit. Its closeness to the Sun makes it the most difficult of the brighter planets to observe with the naked eye in temperate latitudes where long twilight occurs. Because of its rapid revolution round the Sun, its movement adjacent to the stars can readily be noticed by day to day observation.

Naked-eye observation is best attempted when Mercury is a morning 'star', when it rises just before the Sun in September or October at a time coincidental with its maximum westward elongation. At this time its brightness will be mag −1·8. For cautionary advice about observing Mercury in daylight refer to the note concerning daylight observations page 128.

Even in large telescopes little can be made out of the surface of Mercury; it is probably very much like the Moon with the surface heavily pock-marked by craters.

Fig. 52   The planets: right, Venus at crescent phase between Greatest Elongation and Inferior Conjunction; below, top, Mars and Jupiter; bottom, Saturn and Pluto.

119

Venus

Venus is the brightest of all the planets, and near eastern elongation it can be picked up with the unaided eye even before the Sun has set. At this time it can also be seen with the unaided eye at midday if one knows *exactly* where to look (*see* page 127). After dark, during its brightest phase, it will cast a perceptible shadow.

Venus is a larger planet than Mercury with a diameter of 12,400 km and an orbital period round the Sun of 225 days. Because it also lies inside the Earth's orbit, it is observed (like Mercury) alternatively as an evening or morning 'star'. When at its brightest it shines at mag −4·4. In the ancient world it was famous in its dual guise of 'Hesperus' and 'Phosphorus'—as the morning and evening 'stars'—before it was realized that it was the same object at different elongations.

Claims are sometimes made that the phases of Venus can be seen with the naked eye, but this claim is highly suspect. However, a pair of 8 × 30 prismatic binoculars will readily show them. Venus and Mercury show variable phases because they revolve round the Sun inside the Earth's orbit. In a telescope the surface is obscured by dense opaque cloud. Investigations using radio-waves have revealed the surface in certain regions to be pock-marked with craters.

Mars

Mars has long been known as 'the Red Planet'. It is the first planet which lies outside the Earth's orbit, and therefore, when nearest to the Earth, presents its entire visible illuminated side (in contrast to Mercury and Venus which, when nearest, show only their dark (night) sides).

Mars has a diameter of 6,800 km, and it takes 1·88 Earth years (or 687 days) to orbit the Sun. When visible at its brightest in the night sky, it can readily be distinguished by its predominantly orange-red colour. Because of its orbital period, it is only close to the Earth (called opposition) once every two years when it shines at mag −2·3. At closest approach a 2-in telescope with × 50 magnification will show the disc with some indistinct markings. With a slightly larger telescope more features are plainly visible, including a polar cap, and the planet's rotation period in about 24 hours can readily be followed.

The surface of Mars is now known to be covered with large craters caused both by volcanoes and by the fall of meteorites. Several features appear to have been eroded like those on Earth, and it has been suggested that running water and ice have played significant roles in shaping the planet's surface.

Asteroids or Minor Planets

Although the majority of asteroids, or minor planets, are tiny bodies, some of the larger ones are occasionally just within range of binoculars and small telescopes. However, to be sure of identifying an asteroid against the backcloth of stars, a chart or atlas showing stars beyond naked-eye visibility is required. Such charts are in *Atlas Coeli*, which depicts stars to mag 7·7, and *Atlas Eclipticalis* or the *Smithsonian Observatory Star Atlas*, which depict stars to mag 9–10. Current positions of the brighter asteroids can be found in popular international astronomical magazines such as *Sky & Telescope* and the various annual handbooks of astronomical societies, some of which are available for consultation at public reference libraries.

Jupiter

This planet is usually very easy to identify without resort to the tables if the observer has a pair of binoculars. It takes twelve years to make one orbit round the Sun and is therefore located in a particular zodiacal constellation for approximately one year's duration.

By the standards of the other planets it is of colossal size with a diameter of 142,800 km. Even simple opera glasses will reveal its four brighter moons (supposing that one or more of them is not in transit or in eclipse behind the planet). With a 2-in or 3-in refractor, the disc of Jupiter (Pl. 12) is seen to be crossed with parallel cloud-belts which have irregularities and spots. The best known feature is called the Red Spot, a semi-permanent feature which varies in colour (but often not red in spite of its name). Using a small telescope, the rotation of the planet in 9 hrs 50 min is readily apparent. After Venus and Mars, Jupiter is the next brightest planet and shines (at opposition) with a magnitude of −2·3.

So far the best views of the planet were obtained by the Voyager probes which in 1979 passed very close to its surface.

Saturn

This is the most famous and popular planet of all to many observers. Almost everyone has heard of the rings of Saturn. Even with binoculars the planet can be seen to have an oval shape, and in a 2-in telescope the form of the rings is distinct. Owing to the changing angle of the rings, due to the planet's revolution round the Sun (in 29·59 years), we see them at different openings.

At its brightest, Saturn appears to the eye as a steady, bright yellowish star of mag −0·2. The surface of the planet is covered in cloud-like belts similar to Jupiter, but less prominent.

Uranus

This was the first of the planets discovered with a telescope, and William Herschel, who made the discovery in 1781, first thought it was a comet. It is really too faint to be seen directly with the naked eye, since it shines at mag 5·8–6·5. With a pair of opera glasses or binoculars it can be picked out from the stars (using *Atlas Coeli* and a current ephemeris). To make anything of a disc it requires a 6-in telescope. Uranus has a diameter of 47,100 km and takes 84·02 years to circle the Sun. Observations with large telescopes have sometimes revealed cloud-like belts vaguely similar to those of Jupiter and Saturn. In 1977 a very faint ring system was discovered around the planet.

Neptune

This planet was discovered in 1846 as the result of a search for an unknown planet after observations showed that Uranus was slightly affected by some unseen body that lay beyond it. At its brightest it shines at mag 7·7, and unless one uses charts like those in *Atlas Eclipticalis* or the *Smithsonian Star Atlas* it is difficult to locate. Particulars about its day to day position are given in several annual handbooks. Neptune has a diameter of about 48,400 km, and it takes 164·8 years to revolve round the Sun.

Pluto

Pluto is the furthest known planet from the Sun, but doubtless some smaller ones exist beyond it, out of range of present-day telescopes. It was discovered in 1930 and requires at least a 15–18-in telescope to see it, since it is never brighter than about mag 14·5. Pluto rotates in 6·3 days, and its orbital period round the Sun is 248·43 years. Its diameter is estimated at about 6,000 km.

Spotting other Celestial Phenomena

Comets

Like the planets, comets generally belong permanently to the solar system. The name comet comes from the Greek word *kometes* meaning 'hairy star' owing to the brighter comets which have long, spectacular naked-eye tails. Even the most inexperienced star spotter will rarely misidentify comets with stars or planets. However, by far the largest number of comets are faint telescopic objects, and some of them are so faint that they can only be photographed using long exposures with the largest telescopes.

Nevertheless, every year or so comets occur which can be seen in binoculars and small telescopes. More rarely there are comets which become spectacular objects to the naked eye. In the recent past such comets were: Ikeya-Seki 1965, Comet Bennett in 1970–1971 and Comet Kohoutek 1973–1974, all of which aroused considerable interest. The Ikeya-Seki Comet was so bright that it could be seen for a time in broad daylight. Comet Ikeya-Seki and Comet Bennett were both discovered by amateur star spotters. Amateurs discover a good many comets, and this is a field of activity where amateur stargazing can bring world fame and immortal glory—since with comets the first discoverer, or if several people discover a comet independently, the first three discoverers have their names attached for all time.

Although competition is very keen in comet discovery, and several amateurs specialize in this activity, the casual star spotter should always be on the look-out for a comet. Owing to their very elongated orbits and their physical characteristics, they are bright near the Sun at perihelion in the evening and morning skies. Amateurs have discovered bright comets quite by accident when looking at other objects; in particular variable star observers occasionally spot a strange nebulous object in the field of view of a variable star. Many bright comets have been discovered by people totally unconnected with astronomy—people who cannot recognize one constellation from another—but they happened to be glancing in the right place at the right time. For example, in 1910, railway workers and diamond miners in South Africa, returning home at the end of a night shift, discovered a spectacular comet in the dawn sky. In 1961, an airline hostess spotted a new comet when looking through the cabin window for the lights of an airport; and there are several instances when airline pilots were the first to spot brilliant comets such as Air France pilot Emilio Ortiz, during a routine flight across the Pacific on 21 May 1970.

Comets must not be confused with meteors (nowadays more correctly called meteroids). It is important to note that although comets do travel with high velocities, the naked-eye observer does not see this directly, and a comet can only be seen to shift by night to night observation. Meteors, on the other hand, flash brilliantly across the sky and generally burn out within a second or so.

The average comet, when observed through binoculars or small telescopes, shows no tail and at first glance cannot be distinguished from a hazy star cluster or nebula. Only watching a suspect stranger for several hours, or from one night to the next, can it be identified by its apparent movement across the starry backcloth. However, some amateur astronomers gain such familiarity with the brighter nebulae and star clusters that any strange new object can be identified at once as a comet.

Meteors (Meteoroids)

Although meteors are colloquially referred to as 'shooting stars', this is only a convenient description, for they have no connection whatsoever with stars. Most meteors are tiny bodies usually smaller than a grain of sand. They are actually tiny particles of cosmic matter revolving round the Sun in orbits like the planets and the comets; in fact there is some connection between comets and meteoroid particles, for they often appear to share common orbits, but how their individual roles are interwoven is not fully understood. Many believe that meteors represent some kind of comet debris; however, there is some evidence which indicates that this may not be the case.

The meteoroids we observe as meteors, or shooting stars, have orbits which happen to intercept the Earth's orbit, or they have orbits which pass sufficiently close to the Earth to be attracted by the Earth's gravitational field. In orbit they are travelling at such high velocities that when they hit the thick blanket of the Earth's atmosphere, the frictional heat produced causes them to burn up long before they have opportunity to reach the ground. Occasionally the Earth encounters a swarm of such bodies which gives rise to a meteor shower or storm. Each year there are a number of such showers (*see* constellation notes) and on much rarer occasions magnificent meteor storms occur (*see* p. 94). Sometimes a bright meteor will leave a persistent train, or trail, in the atmosphere which may last for some time long after the solid meteor itself has burned up.

Fireballs

There is a bright class of object similar to meteors called fireballs (or bolides). These should not be confused with terrestrial fireballs or 'thunderbolts' which are purely local phenomena connected with electrical storms.

A fireball by classification is a meteor brighter than mag −4 (or approximately about as bright as Venus at her most brilliant).

Fireballs are not a rare phenomenon: they are produced by pieces, or chunks, of cosmic material larger than those which produce meteors. Not infrequently,

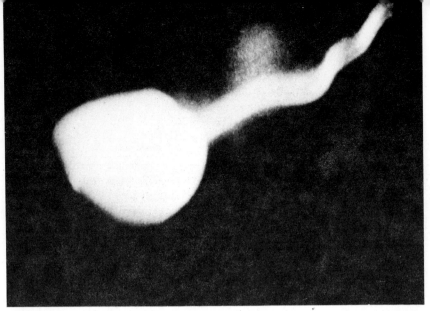

Fig. 53   The great fireball of 24 March 1933 over New Mexico.

if a chunk of material is large enough, it illuminates the night sky to give the effect of broad daylight for a second or so. If the object is sufficiently large, it will not burn up completely and will fall to the ground as a *meteorite* and may cause a crater. Objects of this size give rise to some spectacular noises which witnesses have likened to the thundering of an express train or cannonades; other noises—known as electrophonic noises—may sound like quiet, eerie 'swishings' reminiscent of the effect that wind produces when playing through telegraph wires.

If such an event is witnessed, all the particulars should be carefully noted and written down, for if a meteorite is later found on the ground, interested astronomers will appeal for local eyewitness reports to be sent on to them.

The Zodiacal Light

This is the name given to a 'cone' of light located on or near the ecliptic, above the western horizon after sunset and the eastern horizon before dawn. Its origin is ascribed to a collection, or swarming, of small meteoroid-like particles or dust lying in the plane of the planetary orbits which is rendered visible by reflected sunlight.

In addition there is a second, less conspicuous, component called the Gegenschein, often referred to as the Counter Glow, which lies at a point in the sky opposite the Sun known as the anti-solar point. The chances of seeing the Zodiacal Light depend much on the location of the observer. It is more readily seen at different times of the year and is always better seen in the tropics, especially in remote areas away from urban and city lights. In certain areas of the tropics or subtropics, the Zodiacal Light is so bright that it has been nick-named 'the false dawn' or 'the little daylight'.

Aurora or Auroral Displays

In contrast to the Zodiacal Light the aurora is best seen in high latitudes in both hemispheres. Auroral displays are high atmospheric disturbances caused by electrically charged particles (the Solar Wind) originating from the Sun which interact with the magnetic field of the Earth.

Auroras take the form of sky glows, often with great brilliance running through the whole range of reds, greens and blues in very rapid succession. At the time of sunspot maximum (c. every 11 years), spectacular displays may be seen in the equatorial regions. When aurora is seen in the northern hemisphere, it is called the Aurora Borealis, or Northern Lights; while in the southern hemisphere, it is called the Aurora Australis, or Southern Lights.

In the past the aurora was often confused with large comets; especially suspect are descriptions of ancient comets described by contemporary observers as 'the colour of blood'!

Artificial Satellites and Space Probes

These objects and their carrier rockets are now extremely common in the sky. Many of the brighter ones and their debris can be picked out with the naked eye as they drift across the heavens. Some are deceptively slow-moving and may momentarily startle the star spotter into thinking he has found a nova. Another characteristic is that they may suddenly disappear in mid-sky. This is due to the object passing into eclipse, inside the Earth's shadow, for like the planets, they can only be seen by reflected sunlight, and being located close to us they frequently enter the Earth's shadow zone. The reverse phenomenon is equally startling. To suddenly see a bright object flash into view in mid-heavens never fails to increase the observer's adrenaline flow.

Occasionally with space probes—such as with some of the Apollo series—the gas emission from a rocket propulsion unit may be seen directly. These gas emissions may have the appearance of large, bright, diffuse comets; and sightings like these, plus closely related visible phenomena near military rocket testing sites, frequently give rise to a proliferation of UFO reports from uninformed spectators.

Planet Spotting Tables 1981 – 1993

THE tables which follow enable a planet spotter to locate or identify any of the naked-eye planets between July 1981 and January 1993.

The positions are tabulated at 10-day intervals and are given in *Celestial Longitude*, a coordinate which is measured along the ecliptic to the nearest whole degree. The equatorial deep-sky charts show the plane of the ecliptic (or apparent paths of the planets and the Sun), and along the *top* edge Celestial Longitude is marked off at 10° intervals to coincide with the equivalent hours and minutes of Right Ascension (RA) (for definition *see* p. 24) shown along the bottom edge of the charts. It will be seen that it is a simple matter to convert RA to CL and vice-versa, i.e. 1 hour RA = 15° CL. When the date of observation falls between the tabulated 10-day intervals, a simple fractional estimate is sufficient to locate any planet.

Example: To locate Mars on 24 May 1984, note that the date falls between the entries 19 May 1984 and 29 May 1984. Select the appropriate equatorial deep-sky chart (or key chart) for celestial longitudes 229° and 226° (or alternatively find the correct chart by referring to Table 1 (below) which shows the appropriate CL for different zodiacal constellations (via the Index)). In *soft pencil* lightly plot both longitudes on the chart on the line of the ecliptic and then by fractional proportion mark lightly the estimated position for 24 May.

Example: A strange, bright reddish object is spotted near the ecliptic on 12 October 1988 at the approximate 0° celestial longitude. By resorting to the tables about that date, it will be identified at once as Mars.

From time to time, all the planets vary slightly in their paths along the ecliptic owing to their different orbital inclinations. But the brighter planets will never be more than 7° north or south of the ecliptic (often much less), and they are still sufficiently close to the ecliptic to make recognition easy.

It must be borne in mind that a planet is often located near the Sun and will not normally be visible unless a telescopic or binocular search is made in the daytime sky (*see* daylight observations below and *heed the cautionary warnings*). To assist the planet spotter in deciding whether a particular planet is visible in the night or daylight sky, the position of the Sun is also tabulated at similar 10-day intervals; and this information, when plotted, will provide a ready guide to a planet's suitability for observation in the night sky by bearing in mind its angular relationship to the Sun at any given date.

In the particular case of Mercury it never is greater than about 26° away from the Sun. At its maximum elongation from the Sun it can be observed in daylight with optical equipment (although it is not at its brightest at this time), but extreme caution must be exercised not to look *at* or *anywhere near* the Sun with the naked eye, binoculars or a telescope because of the danger of damaging the eyes. Newcomers to planet spotting are *not* recommended to attempt making daylight observations of Mercury or Venus until they have become familiar with planet spotting in the night or twilight sky *after* the Sun has set.

The list below will assist the observer to quickly locate the zodiacal constellation in which a brighter planet is situated at any particular time by reference to its celestial longitude in the Planetary Tables that follow.

Celestial longitude	Constellation	Celestial longitude	Constellation
0°–26°	Pisces	215°–239°	Libra
26°–50°	Aries	239°–245°	Scorpius
50°–89°	Taurus	245°–265°	Ophiuchus
89°–119°	Gemini	265°–301°	Sagittarius
119°–140°	Cancer	301°–329°	Capricornus
140°–174°	Leo	329°–351°	Aquarius
174°–215°	Virgo	351°–0°	Pisces

Date			Sun	Mercury	Venus	Mars	Jupiter	Saturn
1981	Jul	14	112	91	139	88	183	186
1981	Jul	24	121	104	151	94	185	187
1981	Aug	3	131	123	162	101	186	187
1981	Aug	13	140	144	174	107	188	188
1981	Aug	23	150	163	186	114	190	189
1981	Sep	2	160	179	198	120	192	190
1981	Sep	12	169	194	210	127	194	191
1981	Sep	22	179	206	221	133	196	192
1981	Oct	2	189	213	233	139	198	193
1981	Oct	12	199	212	244	145	200	194
1981	Oct	22	209	200	255	151	202	195
1981	Nov	1	219	200	266	156	204	197
1981	Nov	11	229	212	276	162	207	197
1981	Nov	21	239	228	286	168	209	198
1981	Dec	1	249	244	295	172	211	199
1981	Dec	11	259	260	302	177	212	200
1981	Dec	21	270	275	307	182	214	201
1981	Dec	31	280	292	310	187	216	201
1982	Jan	10	290	307	308	190	217	202
1982	Jan	20	300	318	303	193	218	202

Date			Sun	Mercury	Venus	Mars	Jupiter	Saturn
1982	Jan	30	310	315	297	196	219	203
1982	Feb	9	320	304	293	199	219	203
1982	Feb	19	330	305	295	200	220	203
1982	Mar	1	341	314	299	198	220	203
1982	Mar	11	351	326	306	197	220	202
1982	Mar	21	0	341	314	194	220	201
1982	Mar	31	10	359	323	190	219	200
1982	Apr	10	20	18	334	186	218	199
1982	Apr	20	30	40	344	184	217	199
1982	Apr	30	40	59	355	182	214	198
1982	May	10	49	71	6	180	213	197
1982	May	20	59	75	17	180	212	197
1982	May	30	69	72	29	182	211	197
1982	Jun	9	78	66	40	185	211	197
1982	Jun	19	88	67	52	189	210	197
1982	Jun	29	97	75	64	193	211	197
1982	Jul	9	107	89	76	197	211	197
1982	Jul	19	116	109	88	202	211	198
1982	Jul	29	126	131	100	208	212	198
1982	Aug	8	135	150	112	214	212	199
1982	Aug	18	145	166	124	219	214	199
1982	Aug	28	155	181	137	225	215	200
1982	Sep	7	164	191	149	232	217	201
1982	Sep	17	174	198	162	239	218	202
1982	Sep	27	184	194	174	245	220	203
1982	Oct	7	194	184	187	252	222	204
1982	Oct	17	204	185	199	259	224	205
1982	Oct	27	214	199	212	267	227	207
1982	Nov	6	224	215	224	274	229	208
1982	Nov	16	234	232	237	282	231	209
1982	Nov	26	244	248	249	289	233	210
1982	Dec	6	254	263	262	297	235	211
1982	Dec	16	264	279	274	305	238	212
1982	Dec	26	274	294	287	313	240	213
1983	Jan	5	285	303	299	321	242	213
1983	Jan	15	295	297	312	329	243	214
1983	Jan	25	305	287	325	336	245	214
1983	Feb	4	315	290	337	344	247	215
1983	Feb	14	325	300	350	352	248	215
1983	Feb	24	335	313	2	359	249	215

Date			Sun	Mercury	Venus	Mars	Jupiter	Saturn
1983	Mar	6	345	328	15	7	250	215
1983	Mar	16	355	346	27	15	251	215
1983	Mar	26	5	5	39	23	251	214
1983	Apr	5	15	26	51	30	251	213
1983	Apr	15	25	44	63	37	251	213
1983	Apr	25	35	54	75	45	250	212
1983	May	5	44	55	86	52	249	211
1983	May	15	54	49	97	59	248	210
1983	May	25	64	46	108	66	247	210
1983	Jun	4	73	49	119	73	245	209
1983	Jun	14	83	60	129	80	244	209
1983	Jun	24	92	75	138	87	243	209
1983	Jul	4	102	95	146	94	242	209
1983	Jul	14	111	117	153	101	242	209
1983	Jul	24	121	136	158	107	241	210
1983	Aug	3	130	153	160	113	241	210
1983	Aug	13	140	167	157	120	242	211
1983	Aug	23	150	177	152	127	242	211
1983	Sep	2	159	181	146	133	243	212
1983	Sep	12	169	176	142	139	244	212
1983	Sep	22	179	167	144	145	245	213
1983	Oct	2	189	170	148	141	246	214
1983	Oct	12	198	185	154	158	248	215
1983	Oct	22	208	203	163	164	250	216
1983	Nov	1	218	219	172	170	252	218
1983	Nov	11	228	235	182	176	254	219
1983	Nov	21	239	251	193	182	256	220
1983	Dec	1	249	266	204	188	258	221
1983	Dec	11	259	280	215	193	261	222
1983	Dec	21	269	287	227	199	263	223
1983	Dec	31	279	280	239	204	266	224
1984	Jan	10	289	270	251	209	268	225
1984	Jan	20	300	275	263	214	270	225
1984	Jan	30	310	286	275	219	272	226
1984	Feb	9	320	300	288	224	274	226
1984	Feb	19	330	316	300	228	276	227
1984	Feb	29	340	333	312	232	278	227
1984	Mar	10	350	351	324	235	279	227
1984	Mar	20	360	12	337	238	281	227
1984	Mar	30	10	29	349	239	282	226

Date			Sun	Mercury	Venus	Mars	Jupiter	Saturn
1984	Apr	9	20	37	2	239	282	226
1984	Apr	19	29	34	14	238	283	225
1984	Apr	29	39	28	26	236	283	224
1984	May	9	49	26	39	233	283	223
1984	May	19	58	32	51	229	283	222
1984	May	29	68	45	63	226	282	222
1984	Jun	8	78	61	76	224	281	221
1984	Jun	18	87	81	88	222	280	221
1984	Jun	28	97	103	100	222	279	221
1984	Jul	8	106	123	113	223	277	220
1984	Jul	18	116	140	125	226	276	221
1984	Jul	28	125	152	137	231	274	221
1984	Aug	7	135	161	150	235	274	221
1984	Aug	17	144	163	162	240	273	222
1984	Aug	27	154	156	174	246	273	223
1984	Sep	6	164	149	187	252	273	223
1984	Sep	16	174	155	199	258	273	224
1984	Sep	26	183	171	211	265	274	225
1984	Oct	6	193	190	223	271	275	225
1984	Oct	16	203	207	236	278	276	226
1984	Oct	26	213	223	248	285	277	227
1984	Nov	5	223	239	260	292	279	228
1984	Nov	15	233	253	272	300	281	230
1984	Nov	25	243	265	284	307	283	231
1984	Dec	5	253	271	296	315	285	232
1984	Dec	15	264	262	307	323	287	233
1984	Dec	25	274	254	319	330	289	234
1985	Jan	4	284	261	330	338	292	235
1985	Jan	14	294	273	341	345	294	236
1985	Jan	24	304	287	352	353	297	237
1985	Feb	3	315	303	1	0	299	237
1985	Feb	13	325	320	10	8	302	238
1985	Feb	23	335	338	17	15	304	239
1985	Mar	5	345	357	21	23	306	239
1985	Mar	15	355	13	23	31	308	239
1985	Mar	25	5	19	20	38	310	239
1985	Apr	4	15	13	14	45	312	239
1985	Apr	14	24	7	8	52	313	238
1985	Apr	24	34	8	5	59	314	237
1985	May	4	44	17	7	66	316	236

Date			Sun	Mercury	Venus	Mars	Jupiter	Saturn
1985	May	14	53	30	11	73	317	235
1985	May	24	63	47	18	80	317	234
1985	Jun	3	73	67	26	86	317	234
1985	Jun	13	82	90	36	92	317	233
1985	Jun	23	92	109	46	99	317	232
1985	Jul	3	101	125	56	106	316	232
1985	Jul	13	111	137	67	112	315	232
1985	Jul	23	120	145	78	119	314	232
1985	Aug	2	130	144	89	126	312	232
1985	Aug	12	139	137	101	132	311	233
1985	Aug	22	149	132	113	139	310	233
1985	Sep	1	159	141	124	145	309	234
1985	Sep	11	168	158	136	151	308	234
1985	Sep	21	178	177	148	157	307	235
1985	Oct	1	188	195	161	164	307	236
1985	Oct	11	198	211	173	170	307	237
1985	Oct	21	208	226	186	176	307	237
1985	Oct	31	218	240	198	182	308	238
1985	Nov	10	228	251	211	188	309	239
1985	Nov	20	238	256	223	195	311	240
1985	Nov	30	248	245	236	201	312	242
1985	Dec	10	258	239	249	207	314	243
1985	Dec	20	269	247	261	213	316	244
1985	Dec	30	279	260	274	220	318	245
1986	Jan	9	289	275	286	226	320	246
1986	Jan	19	299	291	299	232	322	247
1986	Jan	29	309	307	311	238	324	247
1986	Feb	8	319	325	324	243	327	248
1986	Feb	18	329	343	336	249	329	249
1986	Feb	28	339	358	349	255	332	250
1986	Mar	10	349	1	1	260	335	250
1986	Mar	20	359	353	14	266	337	250
1986	Mar	30	9	348	26	271	339	250
1986	Apr	9	19	352	39	276	341	250
1986	Apr	19	29	2	51	281	343	250
1986	Apr	29	39	16	64	286	345	250
1986	May	9	48	33	76	290	347	249
1986	May	19	58	53	88	293	349	248
1986	May	29	68	76	100	294	350	247
1986	Jun	8	77	95	112	295	352	246

Date			Sun	Mercury	Venus	Mars	Jupiter	Saturn
1986	Jun	18	87	110	124	295	353	245
1986	Jun	28	96	122	135	294	353	244
1986	Jul	8	106	126	147	291	353	244
1986	Jul	18	115	123	158	285	353	244
1986	Jul	28	125	117	169	283	353	243
1986	Aug	7	134	116	180	282	352	243
1986	Aug	17	144	126	190	282	351	244
1986	Aug	27	154	144	200	283	350	244
1986	Sep	6	163	164	209	285	348	244
1986	Sep	16	173	182	217	288	348	245
1986	Sep	26	183	199	225	293	346	246
1986	Oct	6	193	214	229	298	345	246
1986	Oct	16	203	227	231	304	344	247
1986	Oct	26	213	236	229	310	343	248
1986	Nov	5	223	239	224	316	343	249
1986	Nov	15	233	228	219	323	343	250
1986	Nov	25	243	224	215	329	343	251
1986	Dec	5	253	233	217	336	344	253
1986	Dec	15	263	247	222	343	345	253
1986	Dec	25	273	263	229	350	347	255
1987	Jan	4	284	279	237	357	348	256
1987	Jan	14	294	295	247	4	350	257
1987	Jan	24	304	312	257	11	352	258
1987	Feb	3	314	329	268	18	354	258
1987	Feb	13	324	342	279	25	356	259
1987	Feb	23	334	343	291	32	358	260
1987	Mar	5	344	333	302	39	0	261
1987	Mar	15	354	330	314	46	3	261
1987	Mar	25	4	336	326	52	5	262
1987	Apr	4	14	347	338	59	8	262
1987	Apr	14	24	2	350	66	11	262
1987	Apr	24	34	19	2	73	13	262
1987	May	4	43	39	14	79	15	261
1987	May	14	53	62	25	86	17	261
1987	May	24	63	81	38	92	19	260
1987	Jun	3	72	95	50	98	21	259
1987	Jun	13	82	105	62	105	23	258
1987	Jun	23	91	106	74	112	25	257
1987	Jul	3	101	102	87	118	26	256
1987	Jul	13	110	97	99	124	28	255

Date			Sun	Mercury	Venus	Mars	Jupiter	Saturn
1987	Jul	23	120	100	111	130	28	255
1987	Aug	2	129	112	124	137	29	255
1987	Aug	12	139	130	136	143	30	255
1987	Aug	22	149	151	148	150	30	255
1987	Sep	1	158	170	161	156	30	255
1987	Sep	11	168	186	173	163	29	255
1987	Sep	21	178	201	186	169	28	256
1987	Oct	1	188	214	198	175	27	256
1987	Oct	11	197	222	211	182	26	257
1987	Oct	21	207	222	223	188	24	258
1987	Oct	31	217	211	235	195	22	259
1987	Nov	10	227	209	248	201	21	260
1987	Nov	20	238	220	261	208	21	261
1987	Nov	30	248	235	273	214	20	262
1987	Dec	10	258	251	286	220	20	263
1987	Dec	20	268	267	298	227	20	264
1987	Dec	30	278	282	310	234	20	266
1988	Jan	9	288	299	322	241	20	267
1988	Jan	19	299	315	335	247	21	267
1988	Jan	29	309	327	347	254	22	268
1988	Feb	8	319	326	359	261	24	269
1988	Feb	18	329	315	11	267	26	270
1988	Feb	28	339	314	22	274	28	271
1988	Mar	9	349	322	34	281	30	271
1988	Mar	19	359	334	45	287	32	272
1988	Mar	29	9	349	55	294	35	272
1988	Apr	8	19	6	65	301	37	273
1988	Apr	18	29	26	74	307	39	273
1988	Apr	28	38	48	82	314	42	273
1988	May	8	48	67	87	321	44	273
1988	May	18	58	60	90	327	47	272
1988	May	28	67	86	90	334	49	272
1988	Jun	7	77	85	84	340	52	271
1988	Jun	17	86	79	78	347	54	270
1988	Jun	27	96	77	73	353	56	269
1988	Jul	7	105	84	72	358	58	268
1988	Jul	17	115	97	76	3	60	268
1988	Jul	27	124	116	81	7	61	267
1988	Aug	6	134	138	89	10	63	266
1988	Aug	16	144	157	97	12	64	266

Date			Sun	Mercury	Venus	Mars	Jupiter	Saturn
1988	Aug	26	153	174	107	13	65	266
1988	Sep	5	163	188	117	13	66	266
1988	Sep	15	173	199	128	11	66	266
1988	Sep	25	183	207	139	7	66	267
1988	Oct	5	192	205	150	2	66	267
1988	Oct	15	202	194	162	0	66	268
1988	Oct	25	212	194	174	359	65	268
1988	Nov	4	222	206	186	359	63	269
1988	Nov	14	232	222	198	0	62	270
1988	Nov	24	242	238	211	2	60	271
1988	Dec	4	253	254	223	6	59	272
1988	Dec	14	263	270	235	11	57	273
1988	Dec	24	273	286	248	16	57	275
1989	Jan	3	283	301	260	21	56	276
1989	Jan	13	293	312	273	27	56	277
1989	Jan	23	303	308	286	32	56	278
1989	Feb	2	314	297	298	38	56	279
1989	Feb	12	324	298	311	44	57	280
1989	Feb	22	334	307	323	50	58	281
1989	Mar	4	344	320	336	56	59	282
1989	Mar	14	354	335	348	62	60	282
1989	Mar	24	4	353	1	68	62	283
1989	Apr	3	14	12	13	74	64	283
1989	Apr	13	23	33	25	80	66	284
1989	Apr	23	33	52	38	86	68	284
1989	May	3	43	64	50	92	70	284
1989	May	13	52	67	63	99	72	284
1989	May	23	62	63	75	105	75	284
1989	Jun	2	72	58	87	111	77	283
1989	Jun	12	81	59	100	118	79	283
1989	Jun	22	91	68	112	124	82	282
1989	Jul	2	100	83	124	130	84	281
1989	Jul	12	110	102	137	136	86	280
1989	Jul	22	119	124	149	142	89	279
1989	Aug	1	129	144	161	149	91	278
1989	Aug	11	138	160	172	155	92	278
1989	Aug	21	148	175	184	161	94	278
1989	Aug	31	158	185	196	167	96	278
1989	Sep	10	168	191	208	174	97	277
1989	Sep	20	177	187	219	180	99	277

Date			Sun	Mercury	Venus	Mars	Jupiter	Saturn
1989	Sep	30	187	177	231	187	100	277
1989	Oct	10	197	179	242	194	100	278
1989	Oct	20	207	192	253	200	101	278
1989	Oct	30	217	209	264	207	101	279
1989	Nov	9	227	226	274	213	101	280
1989	Nov	19	237	242	284	220	100	281
1989	Nov	29	247	258	292	227	99	282
1989	Dec	9	257	273	300	234	98	283
1989	Dec	19	268	287	305	241	97	284
1989	Dec	29	278	296	308	248	95	285
1990	Jan	8	288	290	306	255	93	286
1990	Jan	18	298	280	301	262	92	288
1990	Jan	28	308	284	295	269	91	289
1990	Feb	7	318	294	291	276	91	290
1990	Feb	17	328	307	293	284	90	291
1990	Feb	27	339	322	297	291	91	292
1990	Mar	9	349	340	304	298	91	293
1990	Mar	19	359	359	312	306	91	294
1990	Mar	29	8	19	322	313	92	294
1990	Apr	8	18	37	332	321	93	294
1990	Apr	18	28	47	342	328	95	295
1990	Apr	28	38	46	353	335	96	295
1990	May	8	47	40	4	343	98	295
1990	May	18	57	37	16	351	100	295
1990	May	28	67	42	27	358	102	295
1990	Jun	7	76	53	39	5	104	295
1990	Jun	17	86	68	50	12	106	294
1990	Jun	27	95	88	62	19	109	294
1990	Jul	7	105	111	74	26	111	293
1990	Jul	17	114	130	86	33	113	292
1990	Jul	27	124	147	98	40	115	291
1990	Aug	6	133	160	110	46	118	290
1990	Aug	16	143	170	122	52	120	290
1990	Aug	26	153	174	135	57	122	289
1990	Sep	5	162	168	147	63	124	289
1990	Sep	15	172	160	160	67	126	289
1990	Sep	25	182	164	172	71	127	289
1990	Oct	5	192	179	185	74	129	289
1990	Oct	15	202	197	197	75	130	289
1990	Oct	25	212	214	210	74	131	289

Date			Sun	Mercury	Venus	Mars	Jupiter	Saturn
1990	Nov	4	222	230	222	72	132	290
1990	Nov	14	232	245	235	70	133	290
1990	Nov	24	242	260	247	66	133	291
1990	Dec	4	252	273	260	62	133	292
1990	Dec	14	262	281	272	59	133	293
1990	Dec	24	272	273	285	57	132	294
1991	Jan	3	283	264	298	57	132	294
1991	Jan	13	293	269	310	57	131	297
1991	Jan	23	303	281	323	60	129	298
1991	Feb	2	313	294	335	63	128	299
1991	Feb	12	323	310	348	67	126	301
1991	Feb	22	333	327	0	71	125	302
1991	Mar	4	343	345	13	75	124	303
1991	Mar	14	353	5	25	80	124	304
1991	Mar	24	3	22	37	85	123	304
1991	Apr	3	13	30	49	91	123	305
1991	Apr	13	23	26	61	96	124	306
1991	Apr	23	33	19	73	101	125	306
1991	May	3	42	18	84	107	125	306
1991	May	13	52	25	96	112	126	306
1991	May	23	62	38	106	118	128	307
1991	Jun	2	71	54	117	124	129	307
1991	Jun	12	81	74	127	130	131	306
1991	Jun	22	90	97	136	136	133	306
1991	Jul	2	100	117	144	142	134	305
1991	Jul	12	109	133	151	148	136	305
1991	Jul	22	119	146	155	154	139	304
1991	Aug	1	128	154	158	160	141	303
1991	Aug	11	138	156	155	166	143	302
1991	Aug	21	148	149	149	173	146	301
1991	Aug	31	157	142	144	179	148	301
1991	Sep	10	167	149	140	186	150	300
1991	Sep	20	177	165	141	192	152	300
1991	Sep	30	187	184	146	199	154	300
1991	Oct	10	197	201	152	205	156	300
1991	Oct	20	206	218	161	212	157	300
1991	Oct	30	216	233	170	219	159	301
1991	Nov	9	227	247	180	226	161	301
1991	Nov	19	237	260	191	233	162	301
1991	Nov	29	247	265	202	240	163	302

Date			Sun	Mercury	Venus	Mars	Jupiter	Saturn
1991	Dec	9	257	256	213	248	164	303
1991	Dec	19	267	248	225	255	165	304
1991	Dec	29	277	255	237	262	164	305
1992	Jan	8	287	267	249	269	164	306
1992	Jan	18	298	282	261	277	163	307
1992	Jan	28	308	298	274	284	163	308
1992	Feb	7	318	314	286	292	162	310
1992	Feb	17	328	332	298	299	161	311
1992	Feb	27	338	351	310	307	160	312
1992	Mar	8	348	7	323	315	158	313
1992	Mar	18	358	12	335	322	157	314
1992	Mar	28	8	5	348	330	156	315
1992	Apr	7	18	359	0	338	155	316
1992	Apr	17	28	1	12	346	155	317
1992	Apr	27	37	10	25	354	154	317
1992	May	7	47	23	37	1	155	318
1992	May	17	57	40	49	9	155	318
1992	May	27	66	61	62	16	156	319
1992	Jun	6	76	83	74	24	157	318
1992	Jun	16	85	103	86	31	158	318
1992	Jun	26	95	119	98	38	159	318
1992	Jul	6	104	131	111	46	161	318
1992	Jul	16	114	137	123	53	162	317
1992	Jul	26	123	136	135	59	164	316
1992	Aug	5	133	129	148	66	166	315
1992	Aug	15	143	125	160	73	168	314
1992	Aug	25	152	134	173	79	170	313
1992	Sep	4	162	151	185	85	172	312
1992	Sep	14	172	171	197	91	174	312
1992	Sep	24	182	189	210	96	177	311
1992	Oct	4	191	205	222	102	179	311
1992	Oct	14	201	221	234	106	181	311
1992	Oct	24	211	234	246	110	182	311
1992	Nov	3	221	245	258	113	184	312
1992	Nov	13	231	249	270	116	186	312
1992	Nov	23	241	238	282	118	188	313
1992	Dec	3	252	232	294	118	190	313
1992	Dec	13	262	241	305	116	191	314
1992	Dec	23	272	254	317	113	192	315
1993	Jan	2	282	270	328	109	193	316
1993	Jan	12	292	285	339	105	194	317
1993	Jan	22	303	302	350	101	195	318

Appendix 1

THE STARS AS TIMEKEEPERS

When the star spotter has become acquainted with the circumpolar constellations, such as Ursa Major (the Great Bear) and Cassiopeia in the northern hemisphere, and Crux (the Southern Cross) in the southern hemisphere, he has a ready means of telling the time of night.

Northern Stars

Example: Using Ursa Major
Suppose the date to be 28 August (any year).

Looking north, imagine a 12-hour clock face centred on Polaris (α UMi) divided off into separate hours.

Suppose that at the time of observation the pointers (α and β) of Ursa Major stand at the position of '7-o'clock'.

First find Local Star Time (Sidereal Time).

Subtract the time on the Star Clock from 12 hours

$$7 \text{ hrs from } 12 = 5$$
$$\text{Multiply by } 2 = 10$$
$$\text{Add } 11 \qquad = 21 \text{ hrs Local Star Time (Sidereal Time).}$$

Sidereal Time (for definition *see* p. 148) is faster than Civil Time★ (Sun Time) by

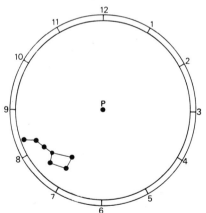

★ Note that Civil Time is strictly Local Time and ignores Daylight Saving Time and convenience times dictated by Zone Times.

4 minutes per day (owing to the Earth's annual revolution round the Sun).

To find Local Civil Time (Sun Time) convert to Local Star Time.

Subtract 2 hours for each month since 23 March and then 4 minutes for each day of the remaining part of the month

in example, date = 28 August
thus 23 March to 23 August = 5 months × 2 hrs
= 10 hrs
23 August to 28 August = 5 days × 4 mins per day
= 20 mins
Total 10 hrs + 20 minutes = 10 hrs 20 mins

Subtract this from Local Star Time (21 hrs − 10 hrs 20 mins) = 10 hrs 40 mins p.m. (Local Time).

Example: Using Cassiopeia
In this method the star Caph (β Cas) is used.

Looking north, imagine a 24-figure clock face centred on Polaris divided into separate hours but numbered in a counter-clockwise fashion.

Read off the number on the circle which corresponds to a fictitious hand connecting Caph to Polaris.

In example shown this = 4.

Add the clock-face number corresponding to the date in the month (I–XII). Thus in example on 1 February (II) = 14.

4 + 14 = 18 hrs = 6 p.m. (Local Time)

If the sum exceeds 24, subtract 24.

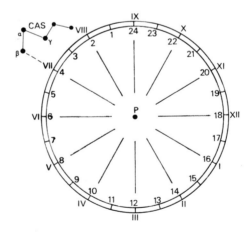

Southern Stars

Example: Using Crux

Looking south, imagine a 24-hour clock face pivoting round α Cru, then use the long axis of the cross and α Cru to γ Cru as the hand.

Read the indicated 'time' and subtract 2 hours for each month and 4 minutes for each day since the last 29 March.

The result is the time *after* midnight on the 24-hour clock.

> Example: Date 31 May
> Indicated time on star clock, 3 hrs
> Borrow 24 hrs
> Therefore 3 + 24 = 27 hrs

29 March to 29 May = 2 (months) × 2 hrs = 4 hrs
29 May to 31 May   = 2 (days) × 4 mins = 8 mins
Subtract 4 hrs 8 mins from 24 hrs = 22 hrs 52 mins
Subtract 12 = <u>10·52 p.m.</u> (Local Time).

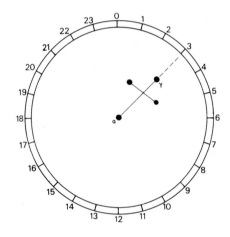

Appendix 2

VARIABLE STARS FOR NAKED-EYE OBSERVATION

Variable		RA 1950·0 h m		Decl 1950·0	Magnitudes Max	Min	Period (days)	Type
TV	Psc	00	25·4	+17°37′	4·6	5·2	49·1	SR
α	Cas	00	37·7	+56°16′	2·5	3·1	—	Irr
YZ	Cas*	00	42·3	+74°43′	5·6	6·0	4·467	EA
γ	Cas	00	53·7	+60°27′	1·6	3·0	—	Irr
o	Cet	02	16·8	−03°12′	2·0	10·1	331·48	LPV
ρ	Per	03	02·0	+38°39′	3·2	3·8	50?	SR
β	Per	03	04·9	+40°46′	2·2	3·5	2·8673	EA
BU	Tau*	03	46·2	+23°59′	5·0	5·5	—	Irr
λ	Tau	03	57·9	+12°21′	3·5	4·0	3·9530	EA
ε	Aur	04	58·4	+43°45′	3·7	4·5	9883	EA
ς	Aur	04	59·0	+41°00′	5·0	5·6	972·162	EA
AE	Aur*	05	13·0	+34°15′	5·4	6·1	—	Irr
α	Ori	05	52·5	+07°24′	0·4	1·3	2070	SR
η	Gem	06	11·9	+22°31′	3·1	3·9	233·4	SR
ς	Gem	07	01·1	+20°39′	4·3	5·1	10·1535	δ Cep
VZ	Cam	07	20·7	+82°31′	4·8	5·2	23·7	SR
U	Hya	10	35·1	−13°07′	4·8	5·8	—	Irr?
R	Hya†	13	27·0	−23°01′	3·5	10·9	387	LPV
δ	Lib*	14	58·3	−08°19′	4·8	5·9	2·3273	EA
χ	Oph	16	24·1	−18°21′	4·4	5·0	—	N
α	Sco	16	26·3	−26°19′	1·2	1·8	1733	SR
g(30)	Her*	16	27·0	+41°59′	4·6	6·0	80	SR
μ¹	Sco	16	48·5	−37°58′	3·0	3·3	1·4463	β Lyr
α¹	Her	17	12·4	+14°27′	3·0	4·0	100	SR
μ	Her	17	15·5	+33°09′	4·6	5·1	2·0510	β Lyr
X	Sgr*	17	44·4	−27°49′	5·0	6·1	7·0122	δ Cep
β	Lyr	18	48·2	+33°18′	3·4	4·3	12·9080	β Lyr
R	Lyr	18	53·8	+43°53′	4·0	5·0	50	SR
χ	Cyg†	19	48·6	+32°47′	2·3	14·3	406·66	LPV
η	Aql	19	49·9	+00°53′	3·9	5·1	7·1766	δ Cep
o¹	Cyg*	20	12·1	+46°35′	4·9	5·3	3803	EA
P	Cyg	20	15·9	+37°53′	3·0(?)	6·0(?)	—	N
T	Cyg*	20	45·2	+34°11′	5·0	5·5	—	Irr
μ	Cep	21	42·0	+58°33′	3·6	5·1	—	SR
δ	Cep	22	27·3	+58°10′	3·9	5·0	5·3663	δ Cep
β	Peg	23	01·3	+27°49′	2·4	2·8	—	Irr
ρ	Cas	23	51·9	+57°13′	4·1	6·2	—	Irr
R	Cas†	23	55·9	+51°07′	4·8	13·6	430·93	LPV

Type Descriptions

SR	Semi-regular stars.
EA	Eclipsing Binary stars of Algol-type.
δ Cep	Delta Cepheid-type variables.
β Lyr	Beta Lyrae-type variables.
Irr	Irregular period stars.
LPV	Long period stars.
N	Novae-type stars.

* Difficult naked-eye object.   † Naked-eye only at maximum.

Appendix 3

THE BRIGHTEST STARS

Star	Apparent Magnitude	Distance (Light Years)
Sirius (α Canis Majoris)	—1·4	8·7
Canopus (α Carinae)	—0·9	181·0
α Centauri	—0·1	4·23
Arcturus (α Bootis)	—0·2	35·86
Vega (α Lyrae)	0·1	26·4
Capella (α Aurigae)	0·2	45·64
Rigel (β Orionis)	0·3	880·0
Procyon (α Canis Minoris)	0·5	11·4
Achernar (α Eridani)	0·6	114·1
β Centauri	0·9	423·8
Betelgeuse (α Orionis)	0·7	586·0
Altair (α Aquilae)	0·9	16·4
Aldebaran (α Tauri)	1·1	68·46
β Crucis	1·5	260·8
Antares (α Scorpii)	1·2	423·8
Spica (α Virginis)	1·2	211·9
Pollux (β Geminorum)	1·2	34·8
Fomalhaut (α Piscis Austrini)	1·3	22·82
Deneb (α Cygni)	1·3	1,630·0
α Crucis	1·1	423·8

THE NEAREST STARS

Star	*Apparent Magnitude*	*Distance (Light Years)*
Proxima Centauri	10·7	4·2
α Centauri A	0·0	4·2
α Centauri B	1·4	4·3
Barnard's Star	9·5	5·9
Wolf 359	13·7	7·6
Lalande 21185	7·5	8·1
Sirius A	—1·4	8·7
Sirius B w	8·7	8·7
Luyten 726–8 A	12·4	8·7
Ross 154	10·6	9·3
Ross 248	12·3	10·3
ϵ Eridani	3·7	10·7
Ross 128	11·1	10·9
Luyten 789–6	12·6	11·0
61 Cygni A	5·2	11·2
61 Cygni B	6·0	11·2
Procyon A	0·5	11·4
Procyon B w	10·8	11·4
ϵ Indi	4·7	11·4
Struve 2398 A	8·9	11·5

w = white dwarf

Appendix 4

ASTRONOMICAL SIGNS AND SYMBOLS

Solar System

☉ Sun
☿ Mercury
♀ Venus
⊕ Earth
♂ Mars
♃ Jupiter
♄ Saturn
♅ Uranus
♆ Neptune
♇ Pluto

- ☾ Moon
- ● New Moon
- ○ Full Moon
- ☽ First Quarter
- ☾ Last Quarter
- ⑤ Minor planet (number in a circle)
- ☄ Comet
- ♈ Vernal Equinox
- ☌ Conjunction
- ☐ Quadrature
- ☍ Opposition
- ☊ Ascending Node
- ☋ Descending Node

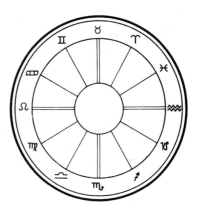

Signs of the Zodiac
*Opposite, clockwise from
the top:* Taurus, Aries,
Pisces, Aquarius,
Capricorn, Sagittarius,
Scorpio, Libra, Virgo,
Leo, Cancer, Gemini.

ASTRONOMICAL UNITS

	Miles (mi)	Kilometres (km)	Astronomical Units (A.U.)	Light Years (l.y.)	Parsecs (psc)
	1	1·6093	$1·076 \times 10^{-8}$	$1·701 \times 10^{-13}$	$0·522 \times 10^{-18}$
	0·62137	1	$0·669 \times 10^{-8}$	$1·057 \times 10^{-13}$	$0·324 \times 10^{-18}$
1 A.U.	$9·29 \times 10^{7}$	$1·495 \times 10^{8}$	1	$0·158 \times 10^{-5}$	$0·485 \times 10^{-5}$
1 l.y.	$5·88 \times 10^{12}$	$9·460 \times 10^{12}$	63,280	1	0·3068
1 psc	$1·916 \times 10^{13}$	$3·084 \times 10^{13}$	206,265	3·260	1

Megaparsec (mpsc) $= 10^{6}$ psc   Kiloparsec kpsc $= 10^{3}$ psc
Velocity of light $= 6·70 \times 10^{8}$ (mi/hr) $= 186,000$ (mi/sec) $= 299,791$ (km/sec)

Temperature Conversion

Units	To	Factor
Fahrenheit (°F)	°C	Subtract 32 and multiply by 5/9
Centigrade (°C)	°F	Multiply by 9/5 and add 32
°C	Kelvin (°K)	Add 273·155

Glossary

Albedo

The percentage of sunlight reflected from a planet or satellite compared with the total amount received from the Sun.

Black Hole

A popular description applied to super collapsed 'stars' (collapsars) whose gravitational attraction is so great that no light can escape their grasp. Such a black hole may occur when a star becomes exhausted of nuclear fuel and collapses under its own weight into a mathematical point to form what is termed a singularity. Essentially all that is left is an intense gravitational field. Such bizarre 'stars' are still conjectural objects, but it is believed that certain X-ray stars consist of a black hole orbiting a normal star—thus forming a very unusual binary system.

δ Cepheids

A class of variable star named after the prototype star δ Cephei. The Cepheids (pronounced 'sefids' or 'sefeeds') are of considerable importance to astronomers in gauging stellar distances. The light fluctuations of these stars proceed with clockwork regularity in periods measured in days. Unlike the eclipsing binary variables such as Algol (p. 81), the Cepheid variations are caused by periodic pulsations in the star itself. When a number of Cepheids had been discovered, a peculiar relationship was noticed between the length of the period of light variations and the luminosity (the intrinsic, or absolute, brightness): the longer the period, the more luminous the star. This period/luminosity relationship, as it is now called, has furnished astronomers with a method of determining stellar distances both in our own Milky Way and in near-by galaxies. It is only necessary to measure the period of a Cepheid in order to deduce its intrinsic brightness, and when this brightness is compared with its *observed* brightness, the distance can be deduced. Today several thousand Cepheid-type variables are known.

Electronic Image Intensifier

A device exploiting the photo-electric effect which enhances the visible signal received from an object in a telescope. Image intensifiers allow optical telescopes to photograph deep-sky objects with shorter exposures and to record faint deep-sky objects normally beyond their range.

Pulsars

A variety of highly condensed stars which are rotating rapidly, possessing intensely powerful magnetic fields. Since their discovery in 1967, over 100 pulsars have been observed by radio telescopes. They emit characteristic 'pulses' of radiation with a clock-like regularity in intervals which range from about 34 pulses a second for the fastest to about 1 pulse a second for the slowest. These pulses are attributed to the star's high-speed rotation, the period of which is actually the true rate of rotation, e.g. a rotation of 34 times per second for the fastest. Pulsars emit radio and X-ray radiation—which is beaconed into space like signals from a high-speed flashing lighthouse.

Pulsars (or neutron stars) like white dwarfs, probably represent stars in a late stage of stellar evolution at a period when nuclear energy is no longer available for burning. Some pulsars are objects visible in optical telescopes, such as the one found in the Crab Nebula (M 1) associated with the supernova seen in A.D. 1054 (see p. 103).

Quasars (Quasi-stellar Objects)

A very unusual class of deep-sky object discovered in the early 1960s which lie at great distances from the Earth. At present there is not satisfactory explanation as to what they represent or to account for their apparent colossal outputs of energy. One theory suggests they are relatively small objects shot out with high velocity by some catastrophic explosive event from our own, or a neighbouring, galaxy. Another theory suggests that quasars are very dense objects intermediate between normal galaxies and black holes. Some quasars and galaxies may be physically connected, but in the Universe as a whole quasars appear to be much rarer objects than galaxies.

Sidereal Time

Literally 'Star Time'; the interval of time measured by the use of stars as reference points. One sidereal day is the time taken by the Earth to rotate adjacent to the position of a particular star = 23 hrs 56 mins = 4 mins shorter than the length of the day measured by the Earth's rotation adjacent to the movement of the Sun.

Additional notes to illustrations

Key to Fig. 14 (p. 32)

Binoculars and accessories useful for star and planet spotting:

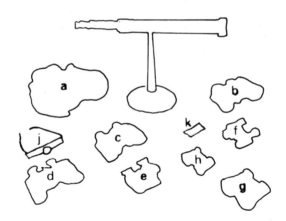

(a) 10×80s (wide field)
(b) 7×35s (wide field)
(c) 8×30s
(d) 6×30s
(e) 7×25s (wide field)

(f) 6×24s
(g) 4×40s (Galilean)
(h) 2×25s (Galilean)
(j) spectacle-type torch
(k) binoc. adaptor for camera tripod

Fig. 42 (p. 89)   The Atlante Farnese globe is the oldest surviving globe show-ing the traditional constellation figures. Note: (left) Centaurus, the Centaur; (centre) Hydra, the Snake; (top centre) Crater, the Cup; (right) Argo, the Ship.

Fig. 46 (p. 103)   This chart of the Pleiades cluster depicts stars to the limit of magnitude *c.* 10–11, some of which are visible in binoculars; in Plate 6 and Jacket Picture the magnitude limit is *c.* 20–1.

Fig. 47 (p. 108)   This Aboriginal bark painting depicts in schematic fashion the Southern Cross (Crux) and the Pointers (α and β) of Centaurus. The legend portrayed concerns the fish *alakitja*. This fish was once part of the Coal Sack (seen to the left of the fish). While swimming in the celestial stream (the Milky Way), it was speared by the two brothers *Wanamoumitja* (α and β Cru) seen above and below the fish. The brothers divided the fish and cooked it, each at his own fire (the two circles δ and γ Cru). Near the brothers are two friends *Meirindilja* (the Pointers α and β Cen), and between them are their boomerangs which they beat to mark time.

Bibliographical Note

For readers seeking a popular introductory guide to general astronomy *see* the author's *Astronomy in Colour* (Blandford Press, London; Macmillan, New York 1974). For readers seeking a comprehensive introductory account of comets, meteorites and meteors *see* the author's *Comets, Meteorites & Men* (Robert Hale, London 1973; Taplinger, New York 1974).

Index to Constellations

Figures in italics indicate principal Key Chart references. Figures in bold indicate principal Deep-Sky Chart references. Note: the genitive ending is included after the abbreviated form.

Index to Stars by Name

General Index

Note: References to colour plate illustrations are printed in bold face type. Figures in italics refer to the page numbers of the black and white illustrations.